HARCOURT
Science

PRE-KINDERGARTEN TEACHER'S GUIDE

Program Advisor

Michael J. Bell
Assistant Professor of Early Childhood
    Education
School of Education
West Chester University
West Chester, Pennsylvania

Program Reviewers

Louise Botko
Cavanagh Early Childhood Center
Crystal, Minnesota

Tanya Copeland
Martin Luther King, Jr. Elementary School
Washington, D. C.

Carnellae W. Davis
Martin Luther King, Jr. Elementary School
Washington, D.C.

Alfreda Di Geronimo
Franklin Township Public Schools
Somerset, New Jersey

Harcourt School Publishers

Orlando • Austin • Chicago • New York • Toronto • London • San Diego

www.harcourtschool.com

Teacher's Guide Contents

Printed in the United States of America

ISBN 0-15-335182-9

2 3 4 5 6 7 8 9 10 021 10 09 08 07 06 05 04 03 02

Using *Harcourt Science* in the Pre-Kindergarten Classroom

The National Science Education Standards state, "In a world filled with the products of scientific inquiry, scientific literacy has become a necessity for everyone." *Harcourt Science* Pre-Kindergarten level gives children a solid base of experiences that form the foundations of scientific literacy.

Goals

The activities, literature, and skill lessons in this book were chosen to help develop children's

- understanding of science concepts.
- science process skills.
- science vocabulary.
- understanding of science inquiry.
- print awareness.
- writing, speaking, and listening skills.

Program Materials

The *Harcourt Science* Pre-Kindergarten program has the following components:

- **Teacher's Guide**–18 lessons for developing science concepts, skills, and vocabulary.
- **Activity Book**–for children to record the results of their investigations. One to five Activity Book pages are included for each lesson.
- **Big Books**–for helping children develop print awareness, vocabulary, and story sense. The large print and colorful illustrations provide a focal point for introducing and discussing key science concepts.
- **Little Books**–sets of five of each title are provided for children to read in a group setting. The small format encourages independent use and review as well.
- **Manipulative Kit**–scientific tools–hand lenses, an observation box, a magnet, and rulers–for hands-on observation and experimentation.
- **Picture Cards**–colorful cards featuring animals and the seasons for use in activities and for independent review.

Organization

This book is organized into three units, one for each of the major strands of science: life science, earth science, and physical science. The lessons are not meant to be completed in one day, but are written to allow you to easily adapt the lessons to your specific schedules and classes. The lessons can also be taught in any order, at any time during the year.

The Lesson Plan

Circle Time

Each lesson begins with *Circle Time*. This provides an opportunity to gather children together to introduce a science concept with the use of a Big Book, fingerplay, action rhyme, or poem. *Circle Time* includes *Use Science Words*, a step-by-step vocabulary building activity. You may want to review science vocabulary throughout the year by posting the vocabulary on a Word Wall.

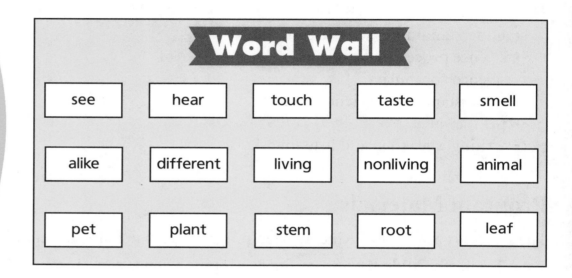

Activity Time

This part of the lesson begins with *Investigate*, a scientific inquiry experience during which children search for answers to a specific question. The activity often calls for the use of scientific tools, such as hand lenses or measuring devices, and concentrates on a science process skill. In the Activity Book, children can record the results of each investigation.

Activity Time continues with *Learn About*. This activity helps develop science concepts as stated in the learning objectives. Program components such as Picture Cards and Little Books are often used in the *Learn About* activities.

Links

Links center activities provide you with a variety of ways to connect science content to other content areas. There is concentration on Language Arts, Math, Social Studies, Art, Music, Health, Drama, and Movement activities.

On the sidebars of the *Links* pages are suggested titles of books and technology programs. A School-Home Connection is also provided, with an activity to help family members feel involved and proactive in their child's first school experiences. You may want to include the activity information in the newsletters or notes you send home with children.

Wrap Up and Assess

Each lesson ends with a group activity to wrap up the lesson, and an individual activity that can be used to assess children's progress. A Portfolio suggestion is also included. Since at this level assessment is often by observation, you may want to record children's development on a short-answer form. A form similar to the one below is easily generated by listing objectives on the blanks and noting the date each objective was accomplished. If preferred, you can use pages that have objectives included, available on Harcourt's Learning Site at **www.harcourtschool.com.** (Go to the Science area of the site.)

Individual Record Form   Pre-Kindergarten Science

Child's Name _____ Larry Singer _____ Teacher _____ Ms. Krieger _____

Unit A: Life Science

Lesson	Objective	Accomplished	Developing	Needs Work	Comments
1	Identify ways people can be alike and different.	9/15			
1	Identify ways to stay healthy.	9/19		9/15	Progressed from one example of staying healthy to three.
1	Identify ways to stay safe.	9/19	9/15		Gave five examples of classroom safety and car safety.
2	Differentiate between living and nonliving things.	9/21			
2	Describe ways that living things are different from nonliving things.	9/21			
3	Identify some ways animals can be grouped.		10/3		

This lesson gives children an introduction to the skills and tools of science emphasized in this program.

Objectives

▶ **Explore senses of sight, smell, taste, touch, and sound by observing objects in the environment.**

▶ **Use science tools to aid in observing and measuring objects.**

Vocabulary

senses	see
hear	touch
taste	smell

Process Skill

observe

Program Materials

Circle Time
  Lots and Lots of Zebra Stripes Big Book
Activity Time
  hand lens
  ruler
  magnet
Wrap Up and Assess
  Activity Book pp. 3–10

Using My Senses to Observe

Circle Time

Hold up the **Big Book** for children and have them preview the photographs. Invite them to predict what the book will be about. Then read the book aloud, giving children plenty of time to observe the photographs on each page. Once you have finished reading, ask children to look around them. Ask: **What patterns do you see?** Help them identify patterns on clothing, books, walls, furniture, and so on.

LOTS AND LOTS OF ZEBRA STRIPES
PATTERNS IN NATURE

Use Science Words

Vocabulary: senses, see, hear, touch, taste, smell

❶ Point out for children that when they look at patterns, they are using their eyes. Model *"seeing"* for children by placing your hands around your eyes as imaginary binoculars. Then ask: **What else can you see in the classroom?**

❷ Expand the conversation to talk about the other *senses*. Say: **You use your eyes to see. What do you do with your nose?** Once children have identified the sense of *smell*, name a variety of fragrant items such as flowers, bread, garbage, and so on, and have children use descriptive words to tell what each smells like.

❸ Repeat the procedure for the senses of *hearing*, *taste*, and *touch*, first having children identify which body part is used for which sense and then describing the sound, taste, and feel of different items you name.

❹ Finally, explain to children that when they see, hear, touch, taste, or smell something, they are using their senses to observe it. Then have children fill in the blanks and motion along as you say:

I *see* with my _____.   (Point to eyes.)
I *hear* with my _____.   (Point to ears.)
I *smell* with my _____.   (Point to nose.)
I *taste* with my _____.   (Point to mouth.)
I *touch* with my _____.   (Shake hands in air.)

Activity Time

Investigate

How can science tools help me observe?

Materials: assortment of science tools such as **hand lenses, rulers, magnets,** thermometers

❶ Place the science tools on a table and invite children to explore them. Have them share ideas about what each tool is used for. Explain what each tool is called and demonstrate how it is used. You may need to teach children how to use a **hand lens.** Tell them to hold the lens near the eye, and adjust the position of the object to be viewed until it comes into focus.

❷ Lead children in a discussion about how the tools help us use our senses. Point out that the hand lens helps us see things close-up, the **ruler** helps us measure things, and so on.

Learn About

Patterns

Materials: blocks in various colors, *Lots and Lots of Zebra Stripes* **Big Book**

Invite pairs of children to demonstrate pattern-making. Have one child place colored blocks in a row to make a pattern. The other child should make the same pattern with another set of blocks. Ask children to tell about the patterns they made. Then reread the **Big Book** and discuss the patterns shown in the pictures.

Reading Corner

▶ **My Five Senses** by Margaret Miller, Simon & Schuster, 1994.

▶ **My Senses** by C.E. Bear, Harcourt, 2001.

▶ **Senses** by Henry Pluckrose, Steck Vaughn Company, 1998.

▶ **Stop, Look & Listen** by Sarah A. Williamson, Williamson Publishing, 1996.

Wrap Up and Assess

▶ Remind children that whenever they use their senses, they **observe.** Display a picture book or play some music and have children tell what they observe.

▶ Reinforce and extend children's understanding of the senses by having them complete **Activity Book** pages 3–10.

LESSON 1

Objectives

▶ Observe ways in which people are alike and different.

▶ Identify some ways to stay healthy.

▶ Identify some ways to stay safe.

Vocabulary

alike   healthy

different   safe

Process Skills

classify/order

Program Materials

Activity Time
    Activity Book p. 11

Learning About Me

Circle Time

Fingers and Toes

We each have fingers.
We each have toes.
We each have a chinny-chin.
We each have a nose.
We each need to sleep at night
And eat good food each day.
But most of all we need each other
To sing and laugh and play—hooray!

Read the action rhyme to children, and model pointing to the body parts named and then pantomime sleeping and eating. Read the action rhyme again and have children do the movements. As you read the last two lines, have children join hands and raise them above their heads, shaking them as they say "hooray!"

Access children's prior knowledge about likenesses and differences among people. Have two children stand next to each other. Ask: **How are these children alike? How are they different?**

Use Science Words

Vocabulary: alike, different, healthy, safe

❶ Have a conversation with children about foods that help people stay healthy. Ask: **What are some healthful snacks that you enjoy?** Remind them that fruits and vegetables are healthful. Show examples. Then encourage each child to tell about one healthy food in a sentence. You might want to remind them of this discussion at snack time.

❷ Lead children in a discussion about safe playtime behavior. Ask: **How can you be safe when you play? Why is it important to be safe? How can you help others be safe too?** Review classroom safety rules with children. Then have each child tell what he or she does to stay safe each day.

Activity Time

Talk with children about things all people can do to feel their best. Ask: **How do you feel when you get a good night's sleep? How do you feel after you eat a good breakfast? What are some things you can do each day to make sure you feel your best?** Help children understand that even though people can be different in many ways, they can all stay safe, make healthy food choices, and get enough sleep.

How can people be alike and different?

Materials: Activity Book p. 11

1 Remind children of the discussion of likenesses and differences from Circle Time. Then work with children to complete **Activity Book** page 11. Read the instructions at the bottom of the page, and help children **classify** the pictures, sorting the children by size, gender, and hair type.

2 Extend the discussion to talk about other ways people are alike and different. Focus the conversation on physical similarities and differences. Help children understand that everyone is unique in some way and that our differences are what make us special.

Staying Safe

Materials: chart paper, drawing paper, crayons

Help children brainstorm tips for staying safe, such as looking both ways before crossing the street, wearing safety gear when necessary, and listening to trusted adults. Draw and list the tips on a sheet of chart paper.

Have each child draw himself or herself demonstrating one of the tips. Display children's illustrations in the classroom with the list of tips. Refer to it whenever children need help following safety procedures.

 Science Background

In addition to proper eating habits, sleep and exercise are also essential for physical health. Sleep lets both the body and the mind rest. Exercise helps the lungs, blood vessels, and muscles work efficiently. Exercise also helps the body produce *endorphins*, chemicals that are natural painkillers. Sufficient sleep and exercise are also important for maintaining a high energy level and resistance to illness and stress.

 Reaching All Learners

ESL Display magazine or newspaper pictures that illustrate healthful, safe behaviors. Have children tell how the people in each picture are staying safe or healthy.

Links

LESSON 1

Reading Corner

- ▶ **The Edible Pyramid** by Loreen Leedy, Holiday House, 1994.
- ▶ **Going to the Doctor** by T. Berry Brazelton, Addison-Wesley, 1996.
- ▶ **Me and My Body** by David Evans and Claudette Williams, Dorling Kindersley, 1992.
- ▶ **Your Skin and Mine** by Paul Showers, HarperCollins, 1991.

House Center

Act Out Food Choices
Health

Materials: plastic foods

Use plastic foods to discuss with children how to choose a healthful snack. Also demonstrate washing your hands, washing the plastic fruits and vegetables, and cleaning up after yourself. Point out that washing hands and foods gets rid of germs that can make people sick.

Have small groups of children act out making a snack. Help them make healthful food choices, and remind them to "wash" and "clean up" as they play.

Art Center

Make a Families Mural
Art

Materials: butcher paper, drawing paper, crayons

Have each child draw a portrait of his or her family. Encourage each child to tell where he or she is in the portrait and who else is shown. Have an adult label the portraits. Display them on a sheet of butcher paper.

Talk with children about how they resemble other members of their families, using the portraits as references when possible. You may also want to display photographs or magazine pictures of families to reinforce this concept. Help children understand that people in a family often resemble one another.

Movement Center

Share a Stretch
Health

Explain that many people stretch for a few minutes each day to help keep their bodies healthy. Have children stand in the rug or mat area. Invite volunteers to show how they stretch when they wake up in the morning. Then lead children in simple stretches they can do each day, such as touching their toes, reaching for the sky, and wiggling their fingers. You may want to lead children in singing "If You're Happy and You Know It," giving stretching instructions as the verses.

Graph Favorite Fruits and Vegetables

Math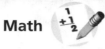

Materials: chart paper, fruit and vegetable shapes cut from construction paper, real fruit (optional)

Remind children that fruits and vegetables are healthful snacks. Talk with them about which fruits and vegetables they like best. Give some examples, such as apples, bananas, oranges, pineapple, cherries, berries, corn, peas, and beans. You may want to show examples of real fruit.

Make a Favorite Fruits and Vegetables pictograph by having each child paste the shape of his or her favorite fruit or vegetable in place on a large grid. Then discuss what the pictograph shows. Which fruit or vegetable is most popular?

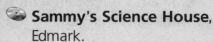
Technology Corner

Demonstrate for children the correct use of a mouse or touch pad. Show them how the devices are properly placed on the desk and clicked or tapped to make a selection. Then use one of these CDs to help reinforce concepts from the lesson:

- **Sammy's Science House**, Edmark.
- **Stickybear's Early Learning Activities**, Sunburst.

School-Home Connection

Have children talk with family members about home safety procedures, such as proper behavior with kitchen appliances and what to do in case of a fire.

Wrap Up and Assess

▶ Have each child dramatize a way to stay healthy or a way to stay safe. Have other members of the group guess what behavior the child is acting out.

▶ Have each child cut two pictures of people out of magazines. Have the child tell one way the two people are alike and one way they are different.

Portfolio You may want to add **Activity Book** p. 11 to children's portfolios.

Objectives

▶ Differentiate between living and nonliving things.

▶ Explore some of the ways that living things are different from nonliving things.

Vocabulary

living   nonliving

Process Skills

observe   compare

Program Materials

Activity Time
Activity Book p. 13

Living and Nonliving Things

Circle Time

Hurt No Living Thing

Hurt no living thing;
Ladybird, nor butterfly,
Nor moth with dusty wing,
Nor cricket chirping cheerily,
Nor grasshopper so light of leap,
Nor dancing gnat, nor beetle fat,
Nor harmless worms that creep.

–Christina Rossetti

Read the poem to children. Encourage them to share their feelings about the poem and the author's message.

Have children name some of the living things mentioned in the poem. Then ask: **What are some other living things? How do you know that those things are living?** Make a list of things children mention.

Name some simple objects that are nonliving, such as rocks, pencils, and books. Have children share ideas about other objects that are nonliving. List these items.

Use Science Words

Vocabulary: living, nonliving

Materials: pictures of living and nonliving things from trade books, magazines, or other sources; paper; glue; crayon

Hold up each picture, first identifying the object as living or nonliving and then having a volunteer tell what the object is. List the names of the objects on a chart. As you finish with each picture, display it in a group with the other living or nonliving things. Once children have **observed** all the pictures, have them glue them to paper, grouping the living and nonliving things on separate sheets of paper. Ask them to **compare** the groups. Ask: **How are the groups alike and how are they different?**

Activity Time

Lead children in a discussion about what *living things* are. Point out that people are living, and have children suggest things that people need to live. Elicit from children that people need food, water, air, and a place to live. Write each word on the board as it is mentioned. Then ask children to name other things they know of that have the same needs. Help them understand that plants as well as animals are living things.

Is a pet a living thing?

Materials: small classroom pet, **Activity Book** p. 13

❶ Review with children that living things need food, water, air, and a place to live. Then have them **observe** the classroom pet for a few minutes and share ideas about whether it is living or not.

❷ Next, point to one of the nonliving things in the pet's environment, such as a rock, shell, or dish. Ask: **Is this a living thing or a nonliving thing? How do you know?**

❸ Have children complete **Activity Book** page 13 for reinforcement.

Real and Made-Up

Materials: *Goldilocks and the Three Bears* and other books with plant and animal characters

Read aloud *Goldilocks and Three Bears.* Say: **Think about *Goldilocks and the Three Bears.* Do real bears talk? Think about *The Three Little Pigs.* Do real pigs build houses?** Help children understand that plants and animals in stories can sometimes do things that real living things cannot do.

Read various trade books with children. After each one, have children identify which characters are like real living things and which do things that show they are made-up.

Science Background

Living things are made up of cells. A cell is the smallest unit of a living thing that is capable of functioning on its own; some organisms, such as bacteria, are made up of only one cell. The human body, on the other hand, is made up of more than a billion cells. There are many different types of cells, but all cells are composed mostly of water. Cells also take in food and excrete wastes.

Reaching All Learners

Challenge   Have children make "Living Things" collages. They can cut out pictures of living things from nature magazines and paste them onto construction paper.

2 Links

Reading Corner

▶ **Alpine Meadow** by Paul Fleisher, Marshall Cavendish, 1999.

▶ **Pick a Pet** by Shelly Rotner and Cheo Garcia, Orchard Books, 1999.

▶ **What's Alive** by Kathleen Weidner Zoehfeld, HarperCollins, 1995.

Outdoors Center

Take a Nature Walk Science

Take children on a short walk through the woods, a neighborhood park, or the school grounds. Help them **observe** and **compare** living things in this environment and talk about the diversity of things they see. Help children identify nonliving things, too, such as rocks, soil, and water. **Caution: Tell children not to touch the living and nonliving things they see.**

Dramatic Play Center

Play Charades Movement

Review some of the living and nonliving things that the class has talked about. Then have children stand in a circle. Have volunteers dramatize living and nonliving things for other children to identify, beginning each dramatization with the statement "I'm thinking of a living thing" or "I'm thinking of a nonliving thing." You may want to model this before children try it.

Art Center

Make a Sponge- Print Tree Scene Art

Materials: crayons; sponges cut into leaf shapes, or real leaves; tempera paint in brown, green, red, orange, and yellow; newsprint

Elicit from children that trees are plants and are therefore living things. Explain that living things grow and change. Trees grow tall and change with the seasons. Have children describe how some trees change in the fall.

Have children paint tree trunks on a sheet of newsprint. Then ask them to add leaves by dipping the sponges into paint and blotting them on the paper. (If you wish, children can use real leaves.) Once the painting is dry, invite children to add other living things in crayon.

I Grew and Changed, Too!

Science

Point out to children that people are living things, too. Remind children that in addition to needing food, water, air, and a place to live, all living things grow and change.

Invite children to bring in photographs of themselves as babies. Display the photographs on a bulletin board in the Game Center. Encourage children to tell about their own baby picture, pointing out their physical features and telling how they grew and changed.

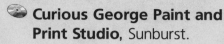
Technology Corner

Have children use the computer and a draw or paint program to create pictures of living or nonliving things discussed in this lesson.

- **Curious George Paint and Print Studio**, Sunburst.
- **Sesame Street Draw and Create in Elmo's World**, Mattel.

School-Home Connection

Have children go on a living/nonliving thing scavenger hunt with family members. Ask them to draw pictures of one living thing and one nonliving thing they found. If cameras are available, children may want to photograph the living and nonliving things and then bring the photographs to school to share.

Wrap Up and Assess

▶ Have children work together to identify all the living things in the classroom. Then have them name as many different nonliving classroom items as possible.

▶ Have children use clay to show one living thing and one nonliving thing that they might see on the way to school.

Portfolio   You may want to add **Activity Book** p. 13 to children's portfolios.

LESSON 3

Objectives

▶ Identify some ways animals can be grouped.

▶ Observe and describe characteristics of animals.

▶ Observe organisms in the classroom and community.

▶ Identify some needs of animals, such as the need for food and water.

Vocabulary

animal   pet
shelter   care

Process Skills

observe   draw conclusions

Program Materials

Activity Time
    Activity Book p. 14
Learn About
    Animal Picture Cards
Links
    What Am I? Little Book
    Animal Picture Cards
    Teacher's Guide, p. 12

Animals

Circle Time

The Puppy

Call the puppy,	(Beckon with finger.)
And give him some milk.	(Pretend to pour milk into bowl.)
Brush his coat	(Make brushing motion.)
Till it shines like silk.	
Call the dog,	(Beckon with finger.)
and give him a bone.	(Hold fingers as if holding a bone.)
Take him for a walk.	(Pretend to hold dog leash.)
Then put him in his home.	(Outline shape of dog house with hands.)

Model the fingerplay for children. Then repeat it, having them do the motions, too. Ask children to share personal experiences with pets. Ask: **What is a pet you have? What does it look like? How do you care for a pet? What do pets and other animals need?**

Elicit from children that different kinds of pets look different and must be cared for in different ways. Dogs, for example, need to be let outside or taken for walks. Birds and hamsters, on the other hand, live in cages and do not go outside. Most animals need food, water, air, light, and a place to live. Point out that most animals do not depend on people for care; instead, they live in nature and take care of themselves. They are sometimes called "wild animals." Ask: **How do animals take care of themselves?**

Use Science Words

Vocabulary: animal, pet, shelter, care

❶ Help children understand that pets are animals that are cared for by people and live in their homes. Talk about what animals make good pets. Point out that some animals, especially animals that need a lot of space or are not used to people, do not make good pets. Have each child name an animal that could be kept as a pet. Write their answers.

❷ Explain that many animals that are not pets still need *shelter*, or places they can go to be safe. Have each child describe a place where an animal might find shelter, such as a nest, a hive, or a burrow.

Activity Time

Encourage children to name as many animals as they can, sharing what they know about where each one lives, what sounds it makes, and what it looks like.

Then have children share ideas about how animals are different from other living things. Point out that, unlike plants, animals can move around on their own; that animal parts are different from plant parts; and that many animals need shelter.

How can we care for a pet?

Materials: classroom pet such as a guinea pig, **Activity Book** p. 14

❶ Review with children some ways people care for pets. Have children **observe** the classroom pet and talk about its care.

❷ Provide the pet with food and water as necessary, and have children **observe** its responses. Ask: **Did the pet eat or drink today? What else can you observe about the pet?** Repeat this process each day for a week.

❸ At the end of the week, have children talk about what they saw. Help them **draw conclusions** about the care the pet needs; they can use **Activity Book** page 14 to record their ideas.

How Animals Can Look Alike and Different

Materials: Animal Picture Cards

Display the **Picture Cards** of adult animals, and discuss ways in which the animals look different. Point out that some animals have no legs while others have two, four, six, or more legs.

Then use the cards to help children identify animals' four basic body coverings: fur, feathers, scales, and skin. Reinforce this idea by having children place each animal card with the card that shows that animal's body covering.

All animals can be scientifically classified according to their physical and biochemical characteristics. An animal is first classified into its *phylum,* the largest subgrouping within the animal kingdom. Animals are then grouped into *classes, orders, families, genera,* and finally *species*. Humans belong to the phylum chordata. Humans are further classified as mammals, primates, hominids, and finally *homo sapiens* (genus and species).

 Reaching All Learners

ESL Use **Animal Picture Cards**, as well as pictures from magazines and trade books, to reinforce the names of different animals. Hold up a picture of an animal and identify the animal. Then have children repeat the animal name a few times. As children gain proficiency, have volunteers identify the animal first, and then have the rest of the children repeat its name.

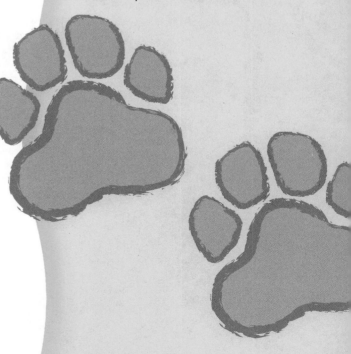

LESSON 3 Links

Reading Corner

- **Animals** by Lucy Floyd, Harcourt, 2000.
- **The Empty Lot** by Dale H. Fife, Sierra Club, 1999.
- **Spots, Feathers, and Curly Tails** by Nancy Tafuri, Greenwillow, 1988.
- **Who Is the World For?** Tom Pow, Walker, 2000.

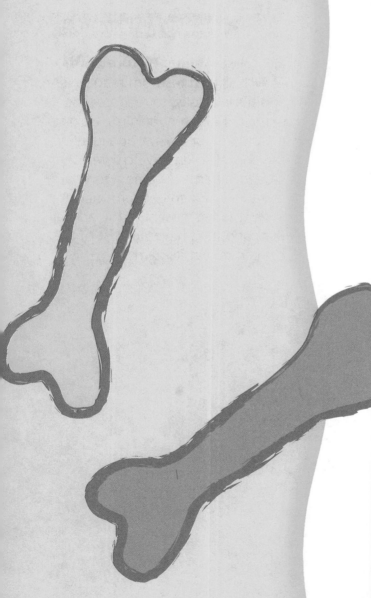

Block Center

Build a Zoo

Science

Invite children to tell about times they have visited zoos, nature preserves, and other places people visit to see animals. Have them tell about the different animals they saw and the kind of space in which each one lived.

Have children work together to build a zoo from blocks. As they do, remind them to think about what would make good spaces for the different animals. A good space for monkeys, for example, might have vines and trees for the monkeys to climb on.

Game Center

Play "What Am I?"

Language Arts

Materials: *What Am I?* Little Book, Animal Picture Cards

Hold up the **Little Book** *What Am I?* Read the title. Have children talk about the cover. Then read the book aloud. Help children guess what animal is shown in each close-up picture. You may want to point out that the animals shown in this book are all insects and that insects are animals, too!

Select the **Animal Picture Cards** that show whole animals and parts of animals. Have children play a game with the cards in which they match each part with the whole animal.

Art Center

Draw an Animal

Art

Materials: crayons, markers, construction paper, craft materials, glue, **Teacher's Guide** p. 12

Review with children some ways in which animals are different, for example in body coverings, size, and way of getting around. Reread the poem on **Teacher's Guide** page 12, "Hurt No Living Thing." Talk about the animals mentioned in the poem. Then have children use construction paper, crayons, and craft materials to make pictures of animals, showing their shape, covering, number of legs, and so on. Invite children to tell about their pictures.

Sing a Movement Song

Music

Talk with children about some of the different ways animals move. Ask questions such as: **How do birds move? How do fish move? How do rabbits move?**

Have children stand in a circle. Sing "Old MacDonald" with them, replacing the animal sounds in the song with animal movements. For example:

Old MacDonald had a farm, E-I-E-I-O.
And on this farm he had a frog, E-I-E-I-O.
With a hop-hop here and a hop-hop there,
Here a hop, there a hop, everywhere a hop-hop…

As you name each movement, have children act it out with you.

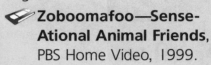

Technology Corner

Have children view a video, such as one of the following, to extend their understanding of the animal kingdom.

Zoboomafoo—Sense-Ational Animal Friends, PBS Home Video, 1999.

See How They Grow: Pond Animals, Sony Wonder, 1995.

School-Home Connection

Have children observe their neighborhoods and tell about the animals they see there.

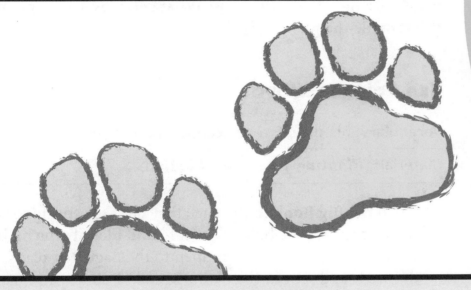

Wrap Up and Assess

▶ Have children work together to make a plan for caring for the class pet. Remind them that their plan should include making sure the pet gets enough food and water.

▶ Give children a sheet of paper folded into thirds. Talk about animals in the sky, animals in the water, and animals on the ground. Have them draw an appropriate animal on each section of the paper. Discuss how the animals are alike and different.

Portfolio You may want to add **Activity Book** p. 14 to children's portfolios.

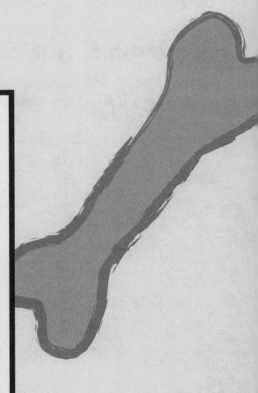

LESSON 4

Objectives

▶ Observe and describe plants in the local environment.
▶ Identify some things plants need to live.
▶ Observe and describe the parts of plants.
▶ Notice similarities and differences among plants.

Vocabulary

plant	stem
soil	seed
leaf	bulb
root	flower

Process Skill

compare

Program Materials

Circle Time
   Planting a Rainbow Big Book
Activity Time
   hand lens
   Activity Book p. 15
Links
   ruler

Plants

Circle Time

Have children share what they know about plants. Ask: **What is a plant? What do plants look like? Where can plants grow? What are the parts of plants?**

Display the **Big Book**. Read the title and have children talk about the cover. Read the Big Book aloud and track the print. Then lead children in a discussion about the various plants shown in the book. Ask: **How were the plants different? What colors were the plants? What made the plants grow?**

Use Science Words

Vocabulary: plant, leaf, root, seed, stem, bulb, flower, soil

Materials: *Planting a Rainbow* Big Book

❶ Open the **Big Book** to the page that says "for spring to warm the soil and sprout the bulbs." Point to and identify the bulbs, flowers, and roots shown. Then open to the page that reads "We sow the seeds and set out the plants in soil." Point to and name the leaves and seeds on these pages. Ask: **Why were the seeds planted in soil?**

❷ Go back through the book and have volunteers point to and identify the bulbs, roots, flowers, seeds, and leaves on each page. Have them notice how the bulbs are alike, how the roots are alike, and so on.

Activity Time

Draw a picture of the following on the board, and identify them for children: tree, shrub, grass, flower, house plant. If possible, show a picture of each. Explain to children that these are some of the different types of plants. Talk about the visible features of each one. Review the **Big Book**, asking children to identify the types of plants that are pictured. Then lead children in a discussion about ways in which all plants are alike.

 **Investigate**

What does a plant need?

Materials: three potted plants of the same type, water, labels, **hand lens, Activity Book** p. 15

1 Label the three plants to match those shown on **Activity Book** page 6. Have children **observe** the plants with the **hand lens.**

2 Put the two plants with *sun* on their labels in a sunny place. Put the plant with only *water* on its label in a dark place. Make sure the two plants with *water* on their labels get enough water.

3 After two weeks, have children **compare** the three plants and record what they see on **Activity Book** page 15.

 **Learn About**

How Plants Are Alike and Different

Materials: drawing paper, crayons

Take children on a short walk around the school grounds. Have them observe different plants in this environment and talk about how each looks. You may want to point out examples of trees, shrubs, grasses, and flowers.

Back in the classroom, have each child draw a picture of one of the plants he or she saw. Display all children's pictures together. Then use the pictures as a basis for discussing how the plants they saw were alike and different.

Each plant part plays a special role in helping a plant meet its needs. *Roots* hold the plant in place. They also take in water and minerals from the soil for the plant. The *stem* moves the water and minerals from the roots to other parts of the plant. It also holds the leaves. *Leaves* use the energy in sunlight and chemicals in the air to make food for the plant. *Flowers* contain the parts of the plant that make seeds for new plants. *Fruits* hold and protect the plant's seeds. Some fruits attract animals that can carry the seeds to new locations. Once a seed has warmth and water, it grows into a new plant.

 Reaching All Learners

Extra Support Display a variety of seeds for children to examine. Have children talk about how the seeds are alike and different. Discuss what happens to the seeds and bulbs pictured in the **Big Book** once they have been planted.

Reading Corner

- **Eating the Alphabet** by Lois Elhert, Harcourt Brace, 1989.
- **From Seed to Plant** by Gail Gibbons, Holiday House, 1993.
- **Paperwhite** by Nancy Elizabeth Wallace, Houghton Mifflin, 2000.
- **The Reason for a Flower** by Ruth Heller, Price Stern Sloan, 1999.

Art Center

Make Leaf Rubbings   Art

Materials: various leaves, tracing paper, crayons

Demonstrate for children how to make rubbings by placing paper on top of a leaf and coloring the paper with a side of a crayon. Then give children leaves, and have them make their own rubbings. (Most children will need help in holding the leaf steady through the paper.) Talk with children about the different leaf shapes and vein patterns shown in the rubbings. Also ask if any shapes are the same.

Dramatic Play Center

Be a Farmer   Science

Talk with children about what farmers do. Elicit that in addition to taking care of animals, many farmers grow plants for food or other purposes. Show an assortment of vegetables or pictures of them.

Have pairs of children dramatize the farmer/plant relationship, with one child being the farmer and the other being a seed or young plant. Ask children to show the farmer caring for the plant and the plant growing. You may want to have children sing "The Farmer in the Dell."

Music Center

Sing a Plant Song   Music

Have children recall that plants need water and light to grow. Then sing the following song with them to the tune of "Mary Had a Little Lamb," demonstrating the actions.

First the farmer plows the ground, (Make plowing motion.)
Plows the ground, plows the ground.
First the farmer plows the ground.
Then he plants the seeds.
This is how he plants the seeds, . . . (Plant seeds.)
So that they will grow.
Rain and sun will help them grow, . . . (Pantomime rain falling and sun shining.)
Right up through the ground.
Now the farmer picks the beans, . . . (Pick the beans.)
And we have food to eat.

Math Center

How Much Did It Grow?

Math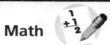

Materials: plant pot, bean seed, soil, water, **ruler**, chart paper

Discuss with children that as many plants grow, they get taller. Have children share ideas about how to find the height of a plant.

Fill the pot with soil, plant the bean seed, and water it. Put the pot in a sunny place. Each day have children observe the growth of the bean seedling. Demonstrate how to measure the height of the plant with the **ruler**, holding the ruler vertically next to the plant and having children count how many inches high the plant is. Keep track of the plant's increasing height on chart paper, making a new entry each day.

Technology Corner

Have children view a video, such as one of the following, to extend their understanding of plants.

Elmo's World: Flowers, Bananas, and Hair, Sony Wonder, 2000.

Franklin Plants a Tree, USA Films, 2001.

School-Home Connection

Have children talk with family members about foods they eat that come from plants. Which plant foods are their favorites?

Wrap Up and Assess

▶ Lead children in a discussion about how plants are alike and different. Have each child suggest one way plants might be **compared**.

▶ Have children draw a plant getting something it needs, such as water or light.

 Portfolio   You may want to add **Activity Book** p. 15 to children's portfolios.

LESSON 5

Objectives

▶ Observe the life cycles of various living things.

▶ Identify ways in which living things resemble their parents.

Vocabulary

adult   born

young   grow

egg

Process Skill

classify/order   communicate

observe

Program Materials

Circle Time
    Moo Moo, Brown Cow Big
    Book
Activity Time
    Activity Book p. 17
    hand lens
    Animal Picture Cards
Links
    My Eggs Little Book

Living Things Grow

Circle Time

Show children pictures of babies. Lead children in a discussion about how animals resemble their parents. Ask: **How do children look like their parents? How do animals look like their parents?**

Show the **Big Book** to children. Read the title, and have children talk about the cover. Then read the book aloud, tracking the print. Stop on each page to have children point out the parent animal and then count the number of young shown. Help children recognize that the young look like their parents.

Use Science Words

Vocabulary: adult, young, egg, born, grow

Materials: sets of labeled flash cards made from drawn or cut-out pictures, each set containing an egg, a young animal, and the corresponding adult animal (use the **Little Book** *My Eggs* for ideas); include one set of cards that shows a chicken egg, a young chicken, and an adult chicken

❶ Initiate a discussion with children about animal life cycles. Ask: **Where does a chicken come from? What is inside a chicken's egg?**

❷ Display the chicken pictures. Point to the egg picture and say *chicken egg.* Point to the chick and say *young chicken.* Point to the adult chicken and say *adult chicken.* Help children understand that a fertilized *egg* has a young chicken inside, a *young chicken* is a chicken that was recently hatched, and *adult* is another way to say *grown-up.*

❸ Display sets of flash cards and have children first identify the animal that is shown and then tell which picture shows the egg, which the young animal, and which the adult. Then have children scramble the cards and **order** them from youngest to oldest.

❹ After Circle Time, place the flash cards in the Science Center for children's independent practice.

Activity Time

Discuss how young animals are different from grown animals. Ask: **Will a young animal always be young? What happens to young animals as they grow?** Help children recognize that young animals grow into adults just as seeds grow into plants.

How does a plant grow?

Materials: seeds, paper towel, potting soil, small containers for planting, **hand lens, Activity Book** p. 17

❶ Sprout the seeds by placing them in wet paper towels for several days. Have children **observe** the sprouted seeds using a **hand lens.**

❷ Give each child a sprouted seed and a planting container. Help children fill the containers with soil, leaving about one inch of space at the top. Help them plant their seeds.

❸ Have children draw pictures each week to **communicate** what their plants look like. Once most seeds have sprouted, have children talk about how their pictures changed. Then have them complete **Activity Book** p. 17.

Animal Young and Their Parents

Materials: Animal Picture Cards

Lead children in a discussion about animal families. Ask: **Could a mouse have an elephant for a mother? Why not?** Help them recognize that young animals come from adult animals of the same kind. Point out that young animals grow up to look like their parents.

Play a matching game with the **Animal Picture Cards.** Place the cards that show adult or young animals face up on a table in random order. Have volunteers match each young animal with its parent. Then have all children identify physical features that the pairs have in common.

 Science Background

Some insects, such as flies and butterflies, undergo metamorphosis as they grow from young animals to adults. In most cases, the process begins with a wormlike larva, hatching from an egg. Eventually the larva changes into a pupa. In this nonfeeding stage of development, the insect undergoes great physical change. Its metamorphosis is complete when it emerges from the pupa case as an adult.

 Reaching All Learners

Extra Support Before reading the **Big Book**, talk about the names people have for some animal young. Point out that a young dog is called a puppy, a young cat is called a kitten, and so on.

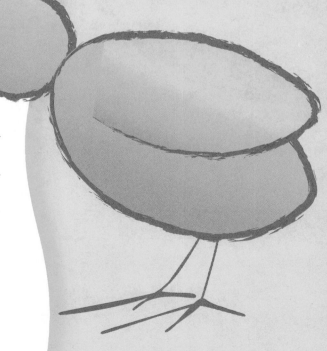

LESSON 5 Links

Reading Corner

▶ **Backyard Sunflower** by Elizabeth King, Viking Penguin, 1994.

▶ **From Caterpillar to Butterfly** by Deborah Heiligman, HarperCollins, 1996.

▶ **Watch Them Grow** by Linda Martin, Dorling Kindersley, 1994.

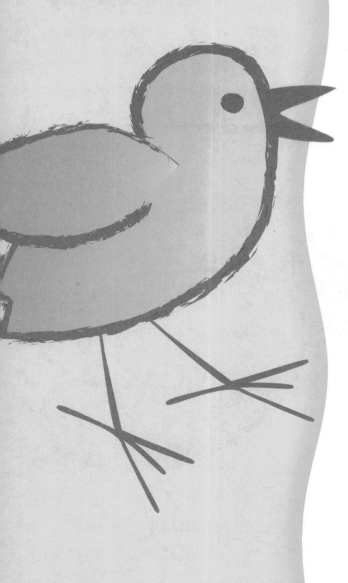

House Center

Taking Care of Baby   Health

Materials: dolls, other household items

Have a discussion with children about why grown-ups must care for babies. Talk about some of the things babies cannot do that older children can do, such as feed themselves, bathe themselves, use the toilet, or walk around. Explain that family members must help a baby do these things until he or she gets bigger. Then invite children to use dolls and other props to act out things someone might do to take good care of a baby.

Language Arts Center

Read About Eggs   Language Arts

Materials: *My Eggs* Little Book

Read the **Little Book** *My Eggs* aloud to a small group, having each child follow along with his or her own book. Have children share ideas about why the parents shown in the book might stay on or near the eggs before they hatch. Then invite each child to draw a picture of one of the parents protecting his or her eggs.

Dramatic Play Center

Hatch from an Egg   Movement

Talk with children about animals that hatch from eggs. Review pictures in the **Little Book** *My Eggs.*

Then lead children in acting out the process of hatching from an egg. Begin by having all children squat on the floor, rolling their heads into their knees tightly and closing their eyes. Have them imagine what it might be like to be curled up tightly inside an egg, not able to see or touch anything on the outside. Then have them slowly "break free" from their eggs. Point out that in real life it might take hours or even days for an animal to hatch completely. Finally, lead children in opening their eyes and stepping from their eggs.

Math Center

Shapes in Order
Math

Materials: flash cards from the Use Science Words activity, construction paper shapes in different sizes (small, medium, large)

Display a set of egg, young animal, and adult animal flash cards in random order. Have a volunteer **order** them from egg to adult. Then display three different-sized circles in random order and encourage a volunteer to **order** them from smallest to largest.

Have children practice putting shapes in order using construction paper shapes from the Math Center. Once they have mastered this, invite them to put the shapes in reverse order from largest to smallest.

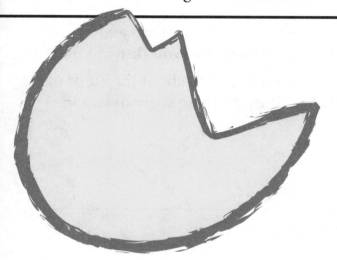

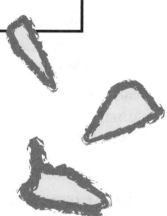

Technology Corner

- Animals at the Zoo (Bobby Susser Songs for Children), 1997.

- Birds, Beasts, Bugs & Fishes Little & Big: Animal Folk Songs, 1998.

- So Big—Activity Songs for Little Ones, 1994.

School-Home Connection

Ask adult family members how they themselves have grown over the years. You may want to prompt discussion by sending home with children a letter with questions such as: **What did you look like when you were a baby? What did you look like when you were [child's name] age?**

Wrap Up and Assess

▶ Lead children in a discussion comparing ways in which different plants and animals grow. Ask: **How did the bean plant change as it grew? How does a caterpillar change?** Help them recall that although plants and animals change in different ways as they grow, most get bigger and do things they could not do when they were smaller.

▶ Have each child draw a young animal with its parent.

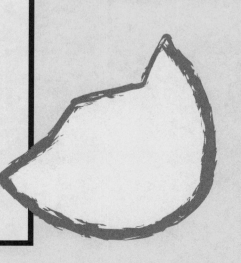

Portfolio You may want to add **Activity Book** p. 17 to children's portfolios.

Objectives

▶ Understand that plants and animals get what they need from their habitats.

▶ Participate in activities that help preserve the environment.

Vocabulary

desert   prairie

ocean   habitat

forest

Process Skill

compare

Program Materials

Activity Time
  Activity Book p. 19
  Animal Picture Cards

Where Plants and Animals Live

Circle Time

Habitats

Some live in the deserts.
Some live in the seas.
Some live on the prairies.
Some live in the trees.

Where do creatures live?
Where it suits them best.
Where they can find water, food,
   and a place to rest.

Have children share what they know about where plants and animals live. Ask: **Where can you find plants? Where can you find animals?**

Read the poem to children, inviting them to talk about the kinds of animals that live in each place. Ask: **Why do these animals live in these places?**

Use Science Words

Vocabulary: desert, ocean, forest, prairie, habitat

❶ Have children recall some of the things plants and animals need to live, such as food, water, air, and shelter. Then explain that plants and animals can live wherever they can get the things they need. The places where the plants and animals live are called *habitats*. Some live in a place made by people, such as a farm or a zoo. Others live in a natural place. Have each child name a place where plants or animals might live.

❷ Then play a question-and-answer game. Ask: **Do plants and animals live in _____?** Name various places that are and are not suitable habitats for plants and animals. For example, forests, shopping malls, oceans, restaurants, and so on. Have children answer *yes* or *no* and explain their thinking.

Activity Time

Review with children some of the habitats discussed earlier in the lesson. If possible, display photographs of various habitats. Then ask children questions such as the following: **What might happen if the [name of habitat] got covered with trash? How can people help keep these places safe?**

Help children understand that keeping habitats safe helps keep plants and animals safe.

How are animal homes alike and different?

Materials: Animal Picture Cards, shoe boxes, craft materials, **Activity Book** p. 19

❶ Divide the class into small groups, and give each group a **Picture Card** that shows an adult animal.

❷ Have children use a shoe box and craft materials to build a habitat for their animal. Remind them to include all the things the animal would need to live.

❸ Display the shoe box habitats. Have children **compare** the habitats, telling how they are alike and how they are different. Children can respond by completing **Activity Book** page 19.

Reusing and Recycling

Materials: recycled and reusable art scraps, scissors, paste

Ask children if their families recycle cans, glass, or newspaper. Tell children that *recycling* something means making it into something new and *reusing* something means using it again. Explain that by reusing and recycling, people help keep plants, animals, and the places they live safe. Tell them that today they will be making pictures out of reused and recycled papers. Then have each child use the art scraps to make collages.

Science Background

When plants or animals cannot get what they need, they may become endangered. One common reason for a species to become endangered is habitat destruction, which makes the land unlivable for plants or animals. Another reason is a drastic climate change that causes the environment to become too wet, too dry, too hot, or too cold for the species to survive.

Reaching All Learners

Extra Support Review information from previous lessons about what plants and animals need to live. Group children in pairs, and have each pair draw a picture of a plant or an animal in its natural environment.

LESSON 6 Links

Reading Corner

- **Charlie Needs a Cloak** Tomie dePaola, Aladdin Paperbacks, 1988.
- **The Empty Lot** by Dale H. Fife, Sierra Club, 1999.
- **The Giving Tree** by Shel Silverstein, HarperCollins, 1986.
- **The Water Hole** by Graeme Base, Harry N. Abrams, 2001.

Art Center

Make an Ocean Mural   Art

Materials: butcher paper, sponges, blue paint, construction paper

Remind children that many plants and animals live in the world's oceans. Have children create an "ocean" in the classroom by sponging blue paint onto the butcher paper until it is almost entirely covered. While the paint dries, have children make ocean organisms such as fish and seaweed by cutting them out of construction paper. Have them paste their ocean plants and animals onto the blue background to create an ocean habitat mural.

Dramatic Play Center

Put on a Puppet Show   Language Arts

Materials: socks, markers, cardboard carton with window cut out of bottom

In advance, make two or three puppets by drawing faces and other features on the old socks. Then have children use the puppets to tell stories they have heard or read.

Movement Center

Explore Hot and Cold   Science

Talk about animals that live in cold places, having children share ideas about how these animals stay warm. Extend the conversation to talk about animals that live in very hot places. Then have children act out different ways people and animals stay warm when the weather is cold and cool when the weather is hot.

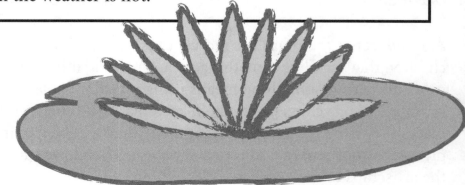

Block Center

Build a Habitat

Science

Materials: blocks

Explain to children that people have habitats, too. Talk about how people get things they need, such as food, warmth, and safety, from their homes and communities.

Have children use blocks from the Block Center to build models of their homes or the community. Encourage children to include the features that help them get things they need, such as sinks for water or grocery stores for food.

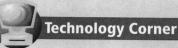
Technology Corner

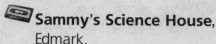
Animals at the Zoo (Bobby Susser Songs for Children), 1997.

Sammy's Science House, Edmark.

School-Home Connection

Have children talk with family members about ways they can reuse and recycle things at home. Children may want to bring to school an object from home that has the symbol for recycling on it.

Wrap Up and Assess

▶ Lead children in a wrap-up discussion by asking questions such as the following: **Where can plants live? Where can animals live?**

▶ Have each child draw a picture of himself or herself reusing something at home or at school. Have children share their drawings with classmates and explain what they show.

Portfolio You may want to add **Activity Book** p. 19 to children's portfolios.

Objectives

▶ Explore features of Earth's surface, such as rocks, soil, and landforms.

▶ Identify sizes, shapes, and colors of various rocks.

▶ Understand that fossils can provide information about living things from long ago.

Vocabulary

land   soil

Earth   mountain

rock

Process Skill

compare

Program Materials

Activity Time
    Activity Book p. 20
    hand lens

Links
    hand lens

Earth's Land

Circle Time

Box of Rocks

I have a rock collection.
I add new rocks each day.
I take long walks to find the rocks
And stow them all away.
I like them dull or shiny;
I like them smooth or rough;
I like them big or tiny—
I'll never have enough!

Introduce the lesson by having children share what they already know about rocks. Ask: **What can rocks look like? What can rocks feel like? Where can you find rocks?**

Read "Box of Rocks" with children. Then have volunteers tell about rocks they have seen, using words from the poem. If any children in the class have rock collections, have them explain where they find their rocks and what features they look for when rock hunting.

Extend the discussion to talk about soil and land in general. Prompt discussion with questions such as: **What does soil look like? What does soil feel like? What is in soil? What does the land around our school look like? Is it flat or hilly?**

Use Science Words

Vocabulary: land, Earth, rock, soil, mountain

Materials: map, pictures of vocabulary words

❶ Discuss the meaning of each vocabulary word with children as you display each picture. Explain that *Earth* is our planet, the place where all people live. Display a map that shows land and water. Explain that *land* is the part of Earth that is not covered with water. Land can have many shapes, such as hills or *mountains*, and is made of *rocks* and *soil*.

❷ To reinforce children's understanding of these terms, say each vocabulary word and have children tell what it means as you display each picture.

Activity Time

Have children examine a globe. Explain that the globe is a model of our Earth. Explain that the blue areas on the globe stand for water and that the brown, green, or multicolored areas stand for land. Point out the United States on the globe, noting its shape, and then point out your home area. Finally, have children share their observations about the globe and the shape of Earth.

What can Earth's land look like?

Materials: large plastic trays, wet sand, **Activity Book** p. 20

❶ Divide the class into small groups, and give each group a tray about half full of damp sand. Have children make a landscape in each tray. Encourage them to include land features they know about such as hills and mountains.

❷ Have children **compare** their landscapes. Ask questions such as the following to prompt discussion: **Is land always flat? What different shapes can land have? Can mountains be different sizes?**

❸ Have children complete **Activity Book** page 20.

Soil

Materials: soil sample in tray, **hand lens**

Ask: **What is under your feet when you walk outdoors?** Accept all responses, but guide children to notice that there is "dirt" or "soil" under their feet. Tell children that you have a sample of soil for them to examine with a **hand lens.** Have children observe and talk about the different bits that make up the soil, such as dirt, twigs, small rocks, and other materials. Make sure children wash their hands after the activity.

Science Background

The total surface area of Earth is nearly 200,000,000 square miles, about 30 percent of which is land. The outermost layer of Earth is the *crust*, which is between 5 and 20 miles thick at any point. Beneath the crust is the *mantle*, which consists of solid rock and reaches temperatures up to 1,800° F. Beneath the mantle lies the *outer core*, which is made of molten iron and nickel and is about 1,400 miles thick. At the center of Earth is the *inner core*, which scientists believe to be made of solid iron and nickel and which reaches temperatures of up to 9,000° F.

Reaching All Learners

Challenge Extend the Learn About activity by having children observe and compare several different types of soil.

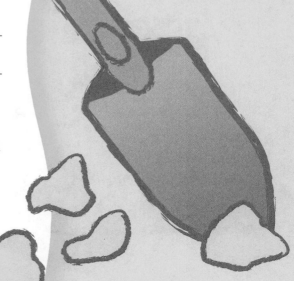

LESSON 7 Links

Reading Corner

▶ **Fossils Tell of Long Ago** by Aliki, HarperCollins, 1990.

▶ **How to Dig a Hole to the Other Side of the World** by Faith McNulty, HarperCollins, 1990.

▶ **Let's Go Rock Collecting** by Roma Gans, HarperCollins, 1997.

▶ **The Magic School Bus: Inside the Earth** by Joanna Cole, Scholastic, 1989.

▶ **Ming Lo Moves the Mountain** by Arnold Lobel, William Morrow, 1993.

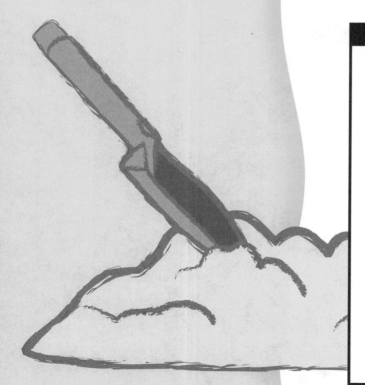

Language Arts Center

Shared Writing
Language Arts

Materials: chart paper, crayons, drawing paper

Write *Earth is* _____. at the top of the chart paper. Lead children in a review of what they have learned about Earth. Then help volunteers complete the sentence frame *Earth is* _____. to write a poem. Record each response on its own line underneath the title. Children can also draw a picture to go with their sentence. Read the entire poem aloud with children.

Table Top Center

Rock Sort
Science

Materials: small rocks, sorting circles, **hand lens**

Have children use **hand lenses** to examine a handful of small rocks. Then have them sort the rocks according to characteristics you name. You might, for example, have children place "big" rocks in one circle and "little" rocks in the other circle. Children might also sort the rocks by texture (smooth/rough) or color (dark/light).

Social Studies Center

Make a Map
Social Studies

Materials: maps, chart paper, markers

Lay out the maps for children to examine. You may want to point out particular landforms or other landscape features that the maps show. Then ask: **How are the maps alike? How are they different? How can people use maps?** Help children understand that maps show where things are.

Take children on a walk around the school grounds, encouraging them to note different features of the area. Then have children help you map the school grounds on chart paper, suggesting different features to include as you draw them in place.

Art Center

Make Handprint Fossils Art

Materials: disposable pie tins, self-hardening clay, toothpicks

Explain to children that sometimes a piece of a plant or an animal gets stuck in soil and, over millions of years, turns into rock. What is left of the plant or animal is called a *fossil*. Tell children that people use fossils to find out what plants and animals were like long ago.

Fill the pie tins with self-hardening clay, making one for each child. Have each child make a handprint in the clay and then engrave his or her name in the clay with a toothpick. Set the tins aside to dry. Once the clay has hardened, loosen and remove it from the tins. Have children talk about how the handprint fossils are alike and different. Send each print home with its owner for family members to enjoy.

 Technology Corner

📀 **This Pretty Planet**, Tom Chapin, 2000.

📀 **The Magic School Bus— Busasaurus**, Atlantic, 1997.

🚌 **School-Home Connection**

With parents' permission, have children start their own rock collections at home. Set aside a time when children can bring their favorite rocks to school for show-and-tell.

Wrap Up and Assess

▶ Ask the class the following questions: **What is land made of? What can land be like?** Have children discuss the responses. Point out any vocabulary words that are mentioned.

▶ Provide children with drawing paper and blue and green crayons. Have each child draw a picture of Earth.

Portfolio You may want to add **Activity Book** p. 20 to children's portfolios.

LESSON 8

Objectives

▶ Understand that water is found on Earth's surface in oceans, lakes, rivers, and ponds.

Vocabulary

ocean   river
lake   pond
stream

Process Skill

observe

Program Materials

Activity Time
    Activity Book p. 21
Links
    Where is Pig? Little Book

Earth's Water

Circle Time

The Sea

Behold the wonders of the mighty deep,
Where crabs and lobsters learn to creep,
And little fishes learn to swim,
And clumsy sailors tumble in.

Discuss bodies of water with children. Show pictures if possible. Encourage them to share personal experiences by asking questions such as the following: **What is a lake? What does a lake look like? What lives in a lake?** Continue by asking the same questions about rivers and streams.

Read the poem aloud to children once. Then have children close their eyes and make a picture in their minds as you read the poem again. Have children describe their mental pictures.

Then ask: **What do crabs and lobsters look like? What is a sailor?** Have children share ideas about other animals or living things that might be found in or near the ocean.

Use Science Words

Vocabulary: ocean, lake, stream, river, pond

Materials: chart paper, markers

❶ Introduce the vocabulary words. As you say each word, have volunteers draw from personal experience to formulate a working definition.

❷ As you discuss each body of water, draw its basic outline. Then have children suggest things to add to the drawing, such as plants, fish, or ducks. Have children compare finished drawings.

Activity Time

Display a globe for children to examine, and have volunteers find parts that represent water. Help them notice oceans, lakes, and major world rivers. Have children observe the shapes and relative sizes of the different bodies of water they see.

 **Investigate**

How does water move?

Materials: water table or tub filled with water; water toys, such as sponges, bottles, pails, and toy boats; **Activity Book** p. 21

❶ Have small groups of children take turns at the water table. Encourage them to move the water in the tub in as many ways as possible, for example, by pouring it from bottles, pushing it with hands, or even blowing on it.

❷ Once children have had a turn, discuss what they **observed**. Ask: **How can you move water?**

❸ Have children respond to the investigation by completing **Activity Book** page 21.

 **Learn About**

Where Earth's Water Goes

Materials: sand table, watering can with shower-type spout, water

Have children make mountains and valleys in the sand. Then make it "rain" over the landscape by pouring water from the watering can.

Have children **observe** where the water goes. Help them understand that some of the water soaked into the sand while some formed streams and puddles, much like rivers and lakes, around the mountains.

 Science Background

All water on Earth is recycled naturally. When water evaporates, it moves up into the atmosphere. Water returns to Earth in the form of rain, snow, sleet, or other precipitation. When water falls to Earth, some of it runs off the land and into streams, rivers, and larger bodies of water. Some water does not run off; instead it soaks into the soil and becomes part of the groundwater supply.

 Reaching All Learners

ESL Give children vocabulary reinforcement by providing pictures of ponds, rivers, lakes, and oceans. Have each child identify what is shown in each picture, using the sentence frame:
This is a _____.

8 Links

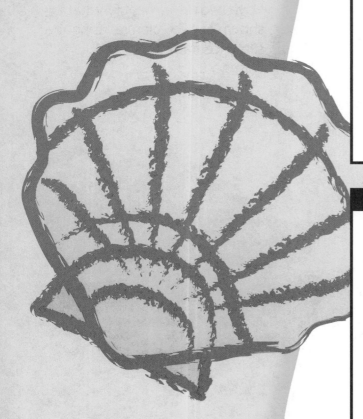

Reading Corner

▶ **Follow the Water from Brook to Ocean** by Arthur Dorros, HarperTrophy, 1993.

▶ **The Ocean Alphabet Book** by Jerry Pallotta, Charlesbridge, 1990.

▶ **River of Life** by Debbie S. Miller, Clarion, 2000.

▶ **Turtle Splash: Countdown at the Pond** by Cathryn Falwell, Greenwillow, 2001.

Language Arts Center

Picture Book

Language Arts

Materials: *Where is Pig?* **Little Book**, drawing paper, crayons or markers

Display the **Little Book,** and read the title aloud. Ask children to predict what the book will be about. Then read the book aloud, tracking the print. Look at the pictures again, and discuss how Pig is enjoying water on each page.

Distribute drawing paper and crayons or markers, and have children make their own picture book. Help children fold the paper in half to make pages. Tell them to show in their book how they enjoy water.

Outdoors Center

Observe a Habitat

Science

Discuss how to stay safe around bodies of water. Then take children on a short field trip to a nearby body of water, or take a video field trip. Have them talk about things they see in this environment, such as rocks, twigs, fish, birds, bugs, and various plants. On returning to the classroom, make a list of observations, and have each child draw a picture of something he or she observed on the trip.

Music Center

Sing a Song

Music

Have children sing a water-related song, such as one of the following:

Row, Row, Row Your Boat

Row, row, row your boat
Gently down the stream.
Merrily, merrily, merrily, merrily
Life is but a dream.

A Sailor Went to Sea

A sailor went to sea, sea, sea,
To see what he could see, see, see.
But all that he could see, see, see,
Was the bottom of the deep blue sea, sea, sea.

Which Holds More?

Math

Materials: containers in various shapes and sizes, colored water, measuring cup, stick-on labels, marker

Have children compare the shapes of the containers. Discuss how much water they think each can hold. Ask questions such as: **Which container do you think can hold the most water? Which can hold the least water?**

With a measuring cup, fill the containers to the top, showing children how much water you are using. Encourage children to count the cupfuls. Label each container. Discuss which container held the most water, which held the least, and whether children were surprised about how much any of the containers could hold. Then have children order the containers according to capacity. You might also have children classify the containers by those that hold more than a cup and those that hold less than a cup.

Technology Corner

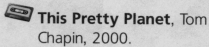 **This Pretty Planet**, Tom Chapin, 2000.

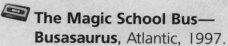 **The Magic School Bus— Busasaurus**, Atlantic, 1997.

School-Home Connection

Suggest that family members provide children with containers, sponges, and water toys at bath time. Encourage children to use bath time to explore water further. You may also want to encourage parents to discuss water safety with their children.

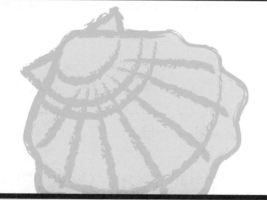

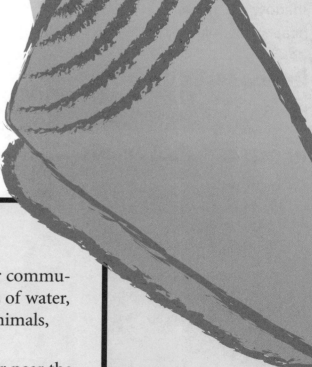

Wrap Up and Assess

▶ Lead children in a discussion about bodies of water in or near your community. Invite children to share experiences with these or other bodies of water, telling about the activities they did there and the kinds of plants, animals, rocks, and soil they saw.

▶ Have each child dramatize the behavior of an animal that lives in or near the water. Children may also wish to act out something that people do in the water, such as sail or swim.

Portfolio You may want to add **Activity Book** p. 21 to children's portfolios.

LESSON 9

Objectives

▶ Observe the sun, noting that it gives off light and heat.

▶ Discuss how the sky changes from day to night.

▶ Predict whether a shadow will change in shape or size with the time of day.

▶ Use nonstandard units to measure shadows.

Vocabulary

sun   day

shadow   night

heat   light

Process Skill

predict

Program Materials

Circle Time
   What is the Sun? Big Book
Activity Time
   Activity Book p. 22

The Sun and Shadows

Circle Time

Lead children in a discussion about the sun. Ask: **What does the sun look like? Where is the sun? What comes from the sun?**

Display the **Big Book,** and read the title. Have children talk about the cover. Read the Big Book aloud, and track the print. Point out both the large and small illustrations. Then reread pages 6–9, the section

of the book that deals with the sun. Help children generate a list of words and phrases that describe the sun, for example *bright, hot, star,* and so on. Then ask volunteers to answer the title question, *What Is the Sun?*, in their own words.

Use Science Words

Vocabulary: sun, light, heat, shadow, day, night

❶ Share the following vocabulary definitions with children: **The *sun* is a star that gives *light* and *heat* to Earth. All living things need the sun. A *shadow* is a dark shape made when an object blocks out the sun's light. *Day* is when we see the sun's light. *Night* is when we do not see the sun's light.**

❷ Remind children of how the boy in the **Big Book** story found out about the sun and moon by asking questions. Ask volunteers to ask their own questions about each of the vocabulary words. You may want to model a possible question for children. Discuss the answers as a group.

Activity Time

Reread pages 6 and 7 of the **Big Book**. Help heighten children's awareness of the sun's importance by having them close their eyes and imagine what life would be like if there were no sun or sunlight. Ask: **How would things be different? How would your day be different?**

How does a shadow change?

Materials: **Activity Book** p. 22

1 In the morning, take children to a sunny area of blacktop on school grounds. Have them spread out in the area, and invite them to observe how their shadows move and change.

2 Then have helpers outline the shadows with chalk. Each child can measure his or her outline by counting how many footsteps long it is. Have children record their measurements on **Activity Book** page 22.

3 Invite children to **predict** whether the shadow will change in size over the course of the day. Return to the sunny spot later in the afternoon, and repeat the procedure. Talk with children about whether their predictions were correct.

Day and Night

Materials: drawing paper, crayons

Talk with children about their favorite daytime and nighttime activities. Invite them to share ideas about what makes certain activities appropriate for the different times. Then have children draw two pictures of themselves, in one doing a daytime activity and in the other doing a nighttime activity. Label the pictures. Have children compare their drawings with those of classmates.

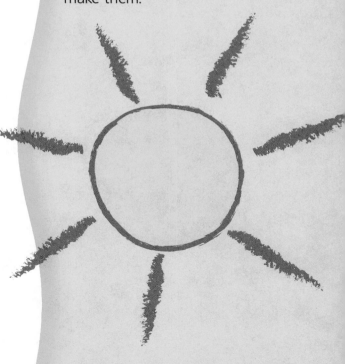

LESSON 9 Links

Reading Corner

▶ **Arrow to the Sun: A Pueblo Indian Tale** by Gerald McDermott, Viking Penguin, 1977.

▶ **Moonbear's Shadow** by Frank Asch, Simon & Schuster, 2000.

▶ **My Shadow** by Robert Louis Stevenson, Candlewick, 1999.

▶ **Shadows and Reflections** by Tana Hoban, Greenwillow, 1991.

Math Center

Clothesline Time Lines   Math

Materials: paper, clothesline, clothespins, markers

Have children tell about their daily routines; what they do when they first wake up, while they are at school, after school, and before they go to bed.

Then have small groups draw pictures that show the different activities. String a clothesline across the classroom. Help each group hang its pictures in order on its own section of clothesline.

Dramatic Play Center

Make Shadow Animals   Movement

Materials: lamp, white sheet

Hang a sheet in the classroom with a lamp placed a few feet behind it. Turn off the main classroom lights, and stand on the lamp side of the sheet, with the children sitting on the other side. Demonstrate for them how you can make shadows on the sheet using your body and hands.

Have several volunteers stand behind the sheet and use their hands, voices, and bodies to imitate different animals for others to guess.

Art Center

Shadow Prints   Art

Materials: dark construction paper, manipulatives such as blocks or counters

Remind children that shadows are made when an object blocks the light. Then have each child arrange some manipulatives on a sheet of dark construction paper. Place the sheets, with the manipulatives on them, in direct sunlight.

Leave the sheets in the light for a week or so. Then have each child remove the objects from his or her sheet and observe the prints made. Invite children to compare their shadow prints with one another.

House Center

Sun Safety

Health

Explain to children that even though the sun provides light and heat for Earth, people must be careful not to get too much sun. Discuss these tips for sun safety:

- **Never look directly at the sun, because it can hurt your eyes.**
- **Wear hats, visors, or sunglasses to keep the sun out of your eyes and off your face on sunny days.**
- **Wear sunscreen or light, long clothing when it is sunny to protect your skin.**

Place items such as hats, visors, sunglasses, parasols, and light summer clothing in the dress-up corner for children to use as you complete this lesson.

Technology Corner

 Great Big Sun, Justin Roberts, 1997.

 Stickybear's Early Learning Activities, Sunburst.

School-Home Connection

Have children go on a "Shadow Hunt" with family members. Invite them to look around their homes and neighborhoods for shadows and talk about the different kinds they see.

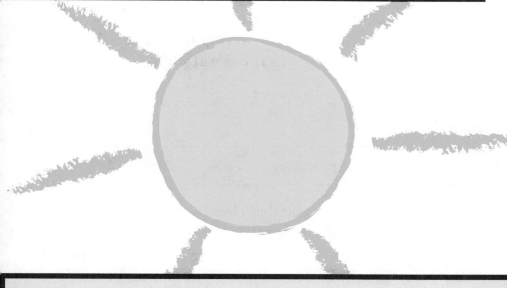

Wrap Up and Assess

▶ Discuss with children why the sun is important. Have each child share one thing he or she learned about the sun, for example, that it provides light and heat for Earth or that plants and animals need the sun.

▶ Have children draw a human figure on a sheet of paper. Tell them where to draw the sun. Then ask them to add a shadow to the pictures in black crayon.

Portfolio   You may want to add **Activity Book** p. 22 to children's portfolios.

Objectives

▶ Observe and describe features of the sky, such as the moon, stars, and clouds.

▶ Understand that the moon can be seen often at night and sometimes during the day.

Vocabulary

cloud   moon

star

Process Skill

draw conclusions

Program Materials

Activity Time
  Activity Book p. 23

The Sky

Circle Time

Stars

At night I see the twinkling stars	(Clasp and open hands.)
And a great big smiling moon.	(Circle arms overhead.)
My mommy tucks me into bed	(Lay two fingers in cupped hand.)
And sings a good-night tune.	(Rock hands back and forth.)

Briefly review with children what they learned in the last lesson about how night and day are different. Have them recall their favorite daytime and nighttime activities. Also ask: **What can you see in the sky during the day? What happens to the sky at night? How does the sky look at night?**

Do the finger play with children, encouraging them to perform it with you. Have them share personal experiences of viewing the night sky. Ask: **What does the moon look like at night? What do the stars look like? What else might you see in the sky at night?**

Use Science Words

Vocabulary: cloud, moon, star

❶ Have children share ideas about what clouds, the moon, and stars may look like in the sky. Elicit that *clouds* may be puffy and white or thick and gray and that they are easier to see during the day; the *moon* usually can be seen at night and looks much larger than the stars; *stars* can be seen at night and their light seems to "twinkle."

❷ Invite volunteers to draw clouds, moons, and stars on the board or a sheet of chart paper. Encourage them to talk about the different sizes and shapes these objects can be.

Activity Time

Lead children in a discussion about the objects they can observe in the night sky. Explain that the moon and sun look larger than the stars because they are closer to Earth.

Why do large objects look small in the sky?

Materials: large playground ball, **Activity Book** p. 23

1 Hold up the ball, and invite children to imagine that it is the moon or a star. Then ask a child to stand in front of the ball as you hold it right in front of his or her eyes.

2 Have the child take one or two steps backward and tell how the ball looks different. Then have the child take several more steps backward, observing how the ball looks smaller and smaller as he or she steps away. Suggest that the child frame the object with his or her hands with each observation.

3 Repeat the process with the other children. Once all have had a turn, invite them to **draw conclusions** about why large objects, such as the moon and the stars, look small in the sky.

4 Have children follow up this activity by completing **Activity Book** page 23.

Clouds

Materials: clipboards, drawing paper, crayons

On a day when clouds are visible, distribute clipboards, paper, and crayons. Then take children outside to observe the sky. As they do so, ask: **How do the clouds look? How do clouds change?** Help children notice that the clouds change shape and move through the sky. Have children draw the clouds they observe. Repeat this exercise on another day, and have children compare their drawings.

Science Background

Though the moon often glows brightly in the night sky, it gives off no light of its own. It reflects the light of the sun. It also does not change shape, as it appears to do; it only reflects the sun's light. The portion of the lit surface that we see depends on the relative positions of sun, moon, and Earth. Earth is about four times larger than the moon. Its circumference is 6,790 miles. Stars give off their own light. They shine all the time but are visible only at night when the sky is clear and dark. They seem to twinkle because we look at them through Earth's atmosphere.

Reaching All Learners

ESL Have children draw pictures to illustrate clouds, moon, and stars. Then, have them point to each illustration and say its name.

10 Links

Reading Corner

▶ **Goodnight Moon** by Margaret Wise Brown, HarperCollins, 1991.

▶ **Moondance** by Frank Asch, Scholastic, 1994.

▶ **Owl Moon** by Jane Yolen, Putnam, 1987.

▶ **Sector 7** by David Wiesner, Houghton Mifflin, 1997.

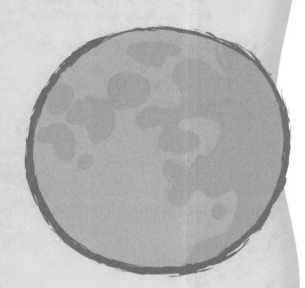

Science Center

Make a Pinhole Star Viewer
Science

Materials: cardboard oatmeal canister with lid removed, ballpoint pen

With the tip of the pen, poke holes in the closed end of the cardboard canister. Have children view the "stars" by pointing the closed end of the canister toward the light and looking through the open end. Or, use a punched sheet of dark paper on an overhead projector. You may also wish to provide children with books that show stars and constellations.

Music and Movement Center

Sing a Nighttime Song
Music

Reread the **Big Book** *What Is the Sun?* Then turn off the lights and lead children in singing "Twinkle, Twinkle, Little Star" and other nighttime songs.

Twinkle, Twinkle, Little Star

Twinkle, twinkle, little star,
How I wonder what you are.
Up above the world so high,
Like a diamond in the sky,
Twinkle, twinkle, little star,
How I wonder what you are.

Art Center

Cloud Paintings
Art

Materials: blue construction paper, white tempera paint, silver glitter, plastic foam trays to hold paint, sponge pieces

Have children recall clouds they have seen and talk about how clouds can look like other things. Then provide them with blue paper and white paint mixed with glitter. Invite them to use sponges to paint different types of clouds — wispy clouds, puffy clouds, big clouds, little clouds, even clouds that look like other things.

Getting Ready for Bed

Health

Talk with children about the different ways people get ready for bed each night. Discuss the nice things about nighttime and talk about what makes them feel safe, warm, and comfortable.

In the House Center, have pairs of children act out bedtime rituals by having one child be the grown-up and the other be the child. Invite the "grown-ups" to help the "children" brush their teeth, wash their faces, and so on. Model this, then allow time for partners to switch roles.

Technology Corner

Bear in the Big Blue House **Vol. 8**, Columbia/Tristar, 1997.

Goodnight Moon, HBO Home Video, 2000.

School-Home Connection

Invite family members to observe the moon with children and help them draw the moon at different times of the month to create a "Moon Journal." At the end of the month, have children bring their journals to school and share what they observed.

Wrap Up and Assess

▶ Make up riddles, such as the following, in which the answer is one of the vocabulary words—*cloud, moon, star*.

I can be fluffy and white or thick and gray.
You can see me best during the day.
What am I?

After children have given answers to the riddles, have them explain the reasons for their answers.

▶ Have each child draw a picture of what the sky might look like at night. Invite children to share their pictures with one another and tell about the different features they drew.

Portfolio You may want to add **Activity Book** p. 23 to children's portfolios.

Objectives

▶ Identify types of weather such as rainy, cloudy, snowy, and windy.

▶ Observe, record, and communicate about each day's weather.

▶ Identify appropriate clothing for different types of weather.

Vocabulary

weather	cloudy
rainy	windy
snowy	sunny
cold	hot

Process Skill

communicate

Program Materials

Activity Time
  Activity Book p. 25

Weather

Circle Time

Rain

Rain on green grass,	(Fingers flutter up and down.)
And rain on the tree,	(Raise hands to form a tree.)
Rain on the roof top,	(Make roof with fingertips.)
But not on me.	(Point to self.)

Ask children to tell what the air is like outside today. Then extend the discussion to talk about other types of weather and how people adapt to them. Ask questions such as: **How do you feel when you are outdoors when it is [type of weather]? What else can it be like outdoors?**

Read the fingerplay once to children without telling them the title. As you read, act out the motions described. Have children tell what they think the fingerplay is about. Then read the title aloud, and tell children to listen carefully as you read the entire fingerplay again.

Use Science Words

Vocabulary: weather, rainy, snowy, windy, cloudy, sunny, cold, hot

❶ Explain to children that *weather* is what the air is like outside. Have a volunteer tell what he or she thinks each vocabulary word means. Encourage other children to add their ideas, too, until a working definition is reached for each word.

❷ Go around the circle and have each child orally complete the following sentence frame: **When the weather is [rainy, snowy, windy, cloudy], I like to _____.** Encourage them to tell what the different types of weather feel like and look like, and to name some activities people do in each.

Activity Time

Review the weather conditions discussed in the Use Science Words activity, and talk about other kinds of weather, such as sunny, foggy, and cloudy. Lead children to also discuss relative temperatures, such as hot, cold, cool, and warm, noting that the weather might be both hot *and* sunny or cold *and* snowy. For each weather condition, have children decide on an appropriate symbol.

How can the weather change in a week?

Materials: chart paper, markers, crayons, **Activity Book** p. 25

1. Begin this project on a Monday. On the chart paper, draw a horizontal five-day calendar. Discuss today's date with children and point out the box that stands for today.

2. Have a volunteer **communicate** the class's ideas about today's weather by drawing a weather symbol in the *Monday* box; then have all children also record this information on **Activity Book** page 25. Repeat this process each day for the rest of the week. (Two weeks may work better, depending on your schedule.)

3. At the end of the week, ask questions such as: **What different kinds of weather did we have this week? What kind of weather did we have the most? How did the weather change?**

Dressing for the Weather

Materials: a variety of warm- and cold-weather dress-up clothes

Lead children in a discussion about ways people dress for the weather. Elicit that light clothes help people stay cool, heavy clothes help people stay warm, and raincoats and umbrellas help people stay dry.

Reinforce these concepts by having children work in small groups to sort the dress-up clothes. Help them sort by asking questions such as: **Which clothes would be good to wear if it were sunny and hot outside? rainy and wet? cold and snowy?**

 Science Background

Scientists who study weather are called *meteorologists*. Meteorologists consider many factors when forecasting the weather, but four of the most important are temperature, air pressure, wind, and humidity. Meteorologists' forecasts not only help people make decisions about what clothes to wear and what activities to plan, they also warn people when dangerous storms are on the way.

 Reaching All Learners

ESL Repeat each vocabulary word for children a few times, emphasizing the /ee/ sound in *sunny, rainy, snowy, windy*, and *cloudy*. Encourage children to identify the shorter word within each vocabulary word (*sun, rain, snow, wind, cloud*). Tell children that they can listen for word parts they do know whenever they need to figure out a word they don't know.

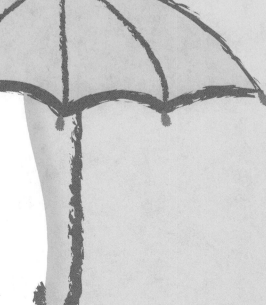

LESSON 11 Links

Reading Corner

- ▶ **Bringing the Rain to Kapiti Plain** by Verna Aardema, Scott Foresman, 1992.
- ▶ **Cloudy with a Chance of Meatballs** by Judi Barrett, Simon & Schuster, 1982.
- ▶ **Rain** by Robert Kalan, Mulberry Books, 1991.
- ▶ **The Snowy Day** by Ezra Jack Keats, Viking Penguin, 1976.

Math Center

Use a Thermometer   Math

Materials: primary thermometer, chart paper, markers

Display the primary thermometer, and tell children how to read it. Explain that the higher the red line is on the thermometer, the warmer the air is outside.

Hang the thermometer in a location where children can see it easily, and then have children observe it each day. Record the temperature each day by drawing and filling in a simple thermometer on the chart paper. At the end of your weather unit, have children use this record to talk about how the temperature changed.

Art Center

Snowy-Day Scenes   Art

Materials: construction paper, glue, cotton balls, crayons

Have children share what they know about snow. Ask questions such as: **What does snow look like? What does snow feel like? When can you see snow? What do people do when it snows?**

Have children make snowy-day scenes by gluing bits of cotton and whole cotton balls onto construction paper. Once the glue is dry, invite children to use crayons to add people, plants, animals, and so on to their scenes.

Dramatic Play Center

Weather Activities   Science

Ask children to describe what they have done or seen other people do in different types of weather. You may want to stimulate discussion by suggesting sledding, flying a kite, and so on. Then say a vocabulary word for a weather type, and let volunteers act out activities they could do in that type of weather.

Sand and Water Center

Explore Sand and Water   Science

Materials: clear plastic jar; sand and water toys, such as plastic bottles, pails, shovels; measuring spoons and cups

Fill the jar with dry sand, and have children examine it. Ask: **Have you ever made mud pies or a sand castle? What do you think will happen if I pour water into the jar? Where will the water go?** Then pour as much water as possible into the jar, showing children how much you are adding as you go. Once no more water can be added, explain to children that between the bits of sand are many tiny spaces where the water goes when it is added to the jar. Explain that just as water you poured seeped into the sand, the water from rain seeps into the ground.

Have children explore water and sand on their own. In particular, you may want to have them observe how dry sand looks and feels and then talk about how the sand changes when water is added.

Technology Corner

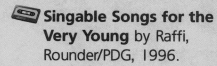
Singable Songs for the Very Young by Raffi, Rounder/PDG, 1996.

The Snowman, Columbia Tristar, 1982.

School-Home Connection

Suggest that family members watch, listen to, or read a weather report with the child.

Wrap Up and Assess

▶ Lead children in a discussion about ways in which weather can change from day to day. Have them share ideas for figuring out what the weather is like when they look outside, for example, by looking at the sky, reading a thermometer, or observing what people are doing and wearing.

▶ Assign each child a type of weather—rainy, snowy, windy, sunny, cloudy, cold, or hot—and have the child draw a picture of himself or herself in that type of weather. Encourage children to show themselves dressed appropriately in their pictures.

Portfolio   You may want to add **Activity Book** p. 25 to children's portfolios.

Objectives

▶ Recognize that animals and plants go through changes as the seasons change.

▶ Observe that changes in weather occur over seasons.

▶ Recognize that seasons occur in a pattern.

Vocabulary

seasons   spring
summer   fall
winter

Process Skills

observe   sort

Program Materials

Circle Time
  Animal Seasons Big Book
  Seasons Picture Cards
Activity Time
  hand lens
  Activity Book p. 26
Links
  Fall Little Book

The Seasons

Circle Time

Invite children to talk about the weather they are experiencing today.

Ask: **What is the weather today? Is it warm or cold? What did the sky look like?**

Then access prior knowledge about the seasons. Ask: **What season is it now? How do you know?**

Explain that a season is a time of the year, and that each season has a certain kind of weather. Many living things change during different seasons.

Display the **Big Book**. Read the title and have children talk about the cover. Then read the Big Book aloud. Encourage a discussion about seasonal changes by asking: **What happened to the flowers in spring? Why did the animals go to cool places in summer? What did the squirrels do in fall? What happened to the rabbit's fur in winter?**

Use Science Words

Vocabulary: seasons, spring, summer, fall, winter

Materials: Seasons Picture Cards, hidden seasonal objects

❶ Hold up a **Seasons Picture Card**, and have children say the name of the season shown. Have them recall an event that happened in the **Big Book** story during that season.

❷ Challenge children to find seasonal objects you have hidden in advance in the classroom. Tell children the season they are looking for, and hold up the appropriate card. Give children verbal clues as they search for the object you are describing.

Activity Time

Talk with children about how they can **observe** the seasons. Remind them of their five senses, and discuss how they can use all their senses to observe. Tell them that one way to observe something carefully is to look at it through a **hand lens**. Remind children how to use a hand lens correctly before doing the next activiy.

How are fall leaves the same and different?

Materials: various sizes, shapes, and colors of fall leaves; **hand lens**; **Activity Book** p. 26

❶ Tell children to choose a leaf to **observe** with the **hand lens**. Suggest that they look for shape, color, texture, and so on.

❷ After they have made their observations, have them draw the leaf on **Activity Book** page 26.

Weather in the Seasons

Materials: 8-inch squares of paper, crayons, **Big Book** *Animal Seasons,* chart paper

Discuss typical weather in each season. Ask children to name their favorite season. Invite them to draw a picture on the square of paper to show the weather in that season. Review the **Big Book** with children to help them get ideas. Then help them make a large graph on chart paper that shows the four seasons. Have them glue their squares into the appropriate row or column. Then ask which season shows the most pictures.

12 Links

Reading Corner

▶ **Changes** by Marjorie N. Allen and Shelley Rotner, Macmillan, 1991.

▶ **How Do You Know It's Fall?** by Allan Fowler, Childrens Press, 1992.

▶ **In For Winter, Out for Spring**, by Arnold Adoff, Harcourt Brace, 1991.

▶ **Summer** by Ron Hirschi, Cobblehill, 1991.

Dramatic Play Center

Seasonal Playlet
Movement

Invite children to bring a stuffed or toy animal from home. Ask them to use what they have learned about animals and the seasons, as well as their imagination, to tell and act out a story about what their animal does during one of the seasons and what the animal will probably do during the next season.

Art Center

Favorite Season Paintings
Art

Materials: tempera paint in foam trays; sponges in various shapes, such as circles, leaves, flowers; paintbrushes; paper

Tell children to think of their favorite season. They should make a painting of the season, using the paint, sponges, and paintbrushes. Model for children how to dip a sponge in paint and press it onto paper. They may want to use a paintbrush to add details.

Language Arts Center

Read Aloud Math
Math

Materials: *Fall* Little Book

Display the **Little Book**, point to the title, and read it aloud. Ask children to tell what they might see outdoors in fall. Page through the book, pointing out the icons and the numbers. Tell children that looking at an icon will help them read the word below it. Discuss how the numbers are symbols for words. Read the book aloud, tracking the print. Then have children read the book aloud with you.

Patterns

Math

Materials: colored blocks, or cubes

Help children understand that a pattern is something that happens or is seen over and over again. Model various simple patterns of colored blocks in a row. For example, one red block, one blue block, one red block. Talk about what block would come next in the pattern. Ask children to make their own patterns of blocks.

Extend and reinforce this idea by discussing events in nature that make a pattern, such as the seasons and day and night.

Technology Corner

 Singable Songs for the Very Young by Raffi, Rounder/PDG, 1996.

 The Snowman, Columbia Tristar, 1982.

 School-Home Connection

Suggest that family members take a walk outdoors with their child to observe and discuss seasonal changes.

Wrap Up and Assess

▶ Ask four volunteers to stand in a circle. Assign each of them a season to represent. Have them name their season as you point to them. Other children should name a change that takes place during that season. Remind children that the seasons occur over and over again in a pattern.

▶ Have children sort the eight **Seasons Picture Cards** into four groups, one group for each season. Ask them to tell why the pictures represent the season.

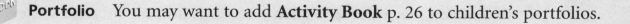

Portfolio   You may want to add **Activity Book** p. 26 to children's portfolios.

LESSON 13

Objectives

▶ Observe and compare properties of objects such as size, shape, color, weight, and texture.

▶ Match a circle, square, and triangle to objects of the same shape.

Vocabulary

size	weight
shape	texture
color	

Process Skill

compare

Program Materials

Activity Time
Bear in a Square Big Book
Activity Book p. 27

Links
The Puppet Show Little Book

Investigating Objects

Circle Time

Display wooden blocks of different shapes and invite children to examine them. Then lead children in a conversation about shapes. Ask: **What shapes do you see here? Tell about each shape. Look around. What are some other shapes you see?**

Hold up the **Big Book** and read the title for children. Then open the book to the first page and have children view the shapes on the yellow background. Invite them to use the book title and this page to predict what shapes they will see in the rest of the book. Read the book with children, tracking the print and discussing the pictures as you go. Then ask: **Where else can you find shapes?**

Use Science Words

Vocabulary: size, shape, color, weight, texture

❶ Pass an ordinary object such as a ball, cup, sock, or book around for children to examine. Encourage children to use their senses to observe the object. Ask: **What color is this? What shape is it? Is it heavy or light? Is it big or small? How does it feel in your hands? What other words tell about it?** You may want to list children's observations.

❷ Repeat the procedure with several other ordinary objects. At this point you may want to explain that *size* is how big or small something is, *weight* is how heavy or light something is, and *texture* is how something feels when you touch it.

❸ Display all the items and invite children to **compare** them. Ask: **Which things are the same color/shape/size? Which things feel the same when you touch or hold them?** Leave the items out for children to discuss further during Activity Time.

Activity Time

Explain to children that when you sort things, you put them into groups. Then have children look once more at the collection of items assembled for Circle Time. Ask: **What groups could we make with these objects?** Help children understand that the items can be sorted by properties that we can see or feel—or observe—such as size, shape, color, weight, and texture.

 **Investigate**

How do objects feel?

Materials: large paper or cloth bag; small manipulatives such as coins, marbles, beads, counters, or fabric swatches; **Activity Book** p. 27

❶ Hold up a few manipulatives and then place them in the bag. Invite a volunteer to put a hand inside the bag and **compare** how the different items feel. Then hold up an item that is identical to one of the items in the bag, and encourage the child to find its match inside the bag without looking. Once the match has been found, have the child explain how the two items feel the same. (**Caution: Be sure children keep the items away from their mouths.**) Give each child a turn.

❷ Have children follow up this activity by completing **Activity Book** p. 27.

 **Learn About**

Matching Shapes

Materials: *Bear in a Square* **Big Book**; circle, square, and triangle shapes cut from construction paper

Reread the **Big Book** with children, taking the opportunity to reinforce the different shape names mentioned in the text.

Hold up the construction paper circle. Encourage children to find other circles in the Big Book and in the classroom. Then repeat the procedure with the triangle and square shapes.

 Science Background

Scientists use a variety of characteristics to describe objects and substances. These are called properties. In addition to size, weight, color, shape, and texture, some other properties are:

mass: the amount of matter in something

density: how heavy or light something is compared to its volume

hardness: how easily something can be scratched by other materials

 Reaching All Learners

ESL Reinforce the names for the different colors by naming several items that are a particular color and then asking children to name others. For example: **This crayon is blue. My pants are blue. The sky is blue. What else is blue?** Or, play "I am thinking of something ___[color]___" with children.

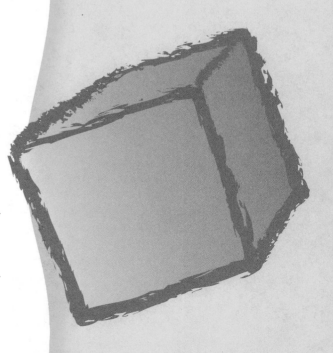

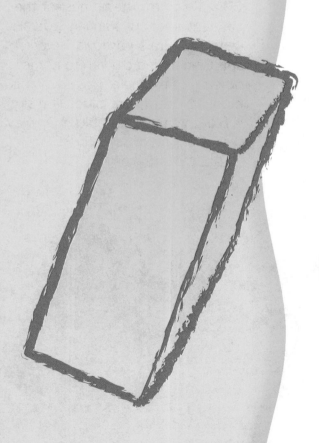

Reading Corner

- **Big and Little** by Margaret Miller, Greenwillow, 1998.
- **Hello, Red Fox** by Eric Carle, Simon & Schuster, 1998.
- **Is a Blue Whale the Biggest Thing There Is?** by Robert G. Wells, Scott Foresman, 1993.
- **Round Is a Mooncake** by Roseanne Thong, Chronicle Books, 2000.

Math Center

Coin Sort
Math

Materials: plastic jar of play coins, including nickels, dimes, pennies, and quarters

Display the four main types of coins for children and have them tell what they know about each one. You may wish to guide the conversation with questions such as: **What shape are the coins? What are coins used for? Why do you think coins are different colors and sizes?** Point out that the coins have different pictures on each side.

Have each child take a handful of coins. Invite children to sort their coins according to type, color, and so on.

Movement Center

A Shoe Game
Science

Have children stand in a circle. Invite children to sort themselves by shoe color, saying: **Who has purple shoes? Stand in the middle!** Have children check one another to make sure that anyone with purple shoes goes to the middle of the circle. Then have the remaining children join hands around those in the middle. Have children repeat the procedure with other shoe colors, saving the most popular colors such as white and brown for last.

Table Top Center

Explore Size
Science

Have children use modeling clay to make pairs of items demonstrating the concept of big and little, such as a small ball and a large ball. Then invite them to make pairs that show other size relationships: thick/thin, long/short, and so on. You may want to make templates in advance, showing examples of the size relationships.

Dramatic Play Center

Texture Puppets

Science

Materials: paper lunch bags, paper and fabric scraps of different textures, **Little Book** *The Puppet Show*

Read the **Little Book** *The Puppet Show* with children and give them time to observe the illustrations closely. Talk with them about how the artist made the pictures. Have them look through the book and tell about the different kinds of paper they see: rough, smooth, speckled, plain, ridged, and colored.

Have children explore the craft materials and talk about how the different materials look and feel. Invite them to make their own puppets by gluing the materials onto paper bags. Then have them work together to put on a puppet show with their new puppets.

Technology Corner

- **Shapes,** School Zone.
- **Stickybear's Early Learning Activities,** Sunburst.

School-Home Connection

Have children and their family members go on shape hunts in their own kitchens. Encourage them to look for common shapes, such as triangles, circles, and squares, in the food they eat, as well as notice any unusual shapes.

Wrap Up and Assess

▶ Have children work in small groups to sort classroom manipulatives by various observable properties.

▶ Have each child bring in a favorite item from home for Show-and-Tell. Encourage children to tell about their items in terms of size, weight, color, shape, and texture.

Portfolio You may want to add **Activity Book** p. 27 to children's portfolios.

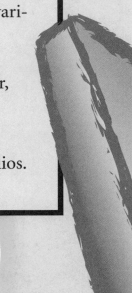

Solids, Liquids, and Gases

Objectives

▶ Observe and communicate three states of matter: solid, liquid, and gas.

▶ Observe and communicate some of the properties of each state of matter.

▶ Understand that air is a gas that is all around us.

Vocabulary

solid   gas
liquid   air

Process Skill

communicate

Program Materials

Activity Time
Activity Book p. 28

Circle Time

Splish, Splash Rain

Splish, splash, the rain falls
In puddles on the ground.
Big ones, small ones, near ones, far ones
Water all around!
I put on my coat and mittens,
I put on my boots and hat.
I jump in all the puddles
To make the water SPLAT!

Invite children to share experiences they have had playing with water, particularly during the "Earth's Water" lesson of the last unit. Ask: **How did you move the water from one place to another? What shape was the water?**

Read the above poem for children, emphasizing the sound words. You may also wish to make motions along with the poem to help children visualize the different actions described. Then lead them in a discussion about water. Ask: **What happened to the water when the author jumped in the puddles? Why?**

Use Science Words

Vocabulary: solid, liquid, gas, air

❶ Provide a wooden block for children to examine. Explain: **This is a *solid*. It keeps its shape. What else holds its shape?** Have children name other materials that keep their shape, pointing out solids in the classroom to reinforce the concept.

❷ Provide a cup of water for children to examine. Explain: **The water is a *liquid*. Liquids change shape when you pour them. What else is a liquid?** Point out that milk and juice are liquids, too.

❸ Hold up a deflated balloon and have children observe how it changes when you blow into it. Then fully inflate the balloon and ask: **What is inside the balloon?** Help children understand that when you blow into the balloon, you are filling it with air. Then explain: **The *air* in the balloon is a *gas*. Gases change shape, too.**

Activity Time

Talk with children about solids, liquids, and gases in their world. Name a variety of everyday objects or substances from home, school, and out-of-doors that children will all be familiar with. Encourage children to identify each as a solid, liquid, or gas and tell how they know.

 **Investigate**

How does water change shape?

Materials: colored water, three clear containers in different shapes, crayons, **Activity Book** p. 28

1. Pour a quantity of colored water into one of the containers. Have each child observe it and draw a picture on **Activity Book** page 28 to **communicate** its shape.

2. Pour the water into another container. Have children observe the new shape of the water and draw a picture of what they see.

3. Pour the water into the third container and have children observe and draw it once more. Invite them to compare their drawings.

 **Learn About**

Air

Materials: water table or pan filled with water, empty plastic bottle

Have children share what they already know about air. Elicit from them that moving air is wind. You might also point out that people breathe air, and illustrate this fact by having children place their hands an inch or so away from their own mouths and feel their own breath as they exhale.

Hold up the empty bottle and ask: **What is inside?** Push the bottle into the water, open mouth down, and then submerge it slowly while keeping the mouth under the water. Tilt the bottle slightly. Point out the bubbles that float up as the bottle fills with water and explain that these bubbles are the air that was inside the bottle. Have children talk about what they see.

 Science Background

Solids, liquids, and gases are all states of *matter*. Matter is what all objects are made of. Scientists define *matter* as anything that has mass and takes up space. There is a fourth state of matter, *plasma*. Most plasmas are found in space. On Earth they form only under carefully controlled conditions.

 Reaching All Learners

Challenge   Inflate a balloon and then let out a little bit of air at a time, allowing children to feel the air as it escapes. Then repeat the procedure, having children listen to the air as it escapes. Encourage them to tell what they felt and heard.

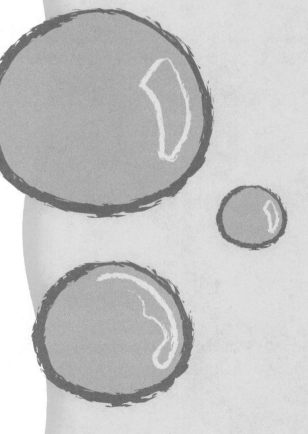

LESSON 14 Links

Reading Corner

▶ **Air Is All Around You** by Franklyn Branley, Harper Trophy, 1986.

▶ **Gilberto and the Wind** by Marie Hall Ets, Penguin Putnam Books for Young Readers, 1998.

▶ **Mouton's Impossible Dream** by Anik McGrory, Gulliver Books, 2000.

▶ **No More Water in the Tub!** by Tedd Arnold, Puffin, 1998.

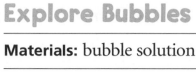

Outdoors Center

Explore Bubbles
Science

Materials: bubble solution

Take children outside on a breezy day and blow some bubbles using the solution. Have children observe the way the bubbles float in the air. Ask: **What is inside the bubbles? What makes the bubbles float around?** Help children understand that air is what fills the bubbles and what pushes them around. Invite children to blow their own bubbles and to observe what the bubbles do.

Art Center

Solid Sculptures
Art

Materials: self-hardening clay

Invite children to hold a lump of clay in their hands and talk about how it feels. Ask: **Is the clay a solid, liquid, or gas? Why do you think so?**

Have each child make a sculpture using a small lump of the clay. Show some examples, and tell children that their sculptures can show real or made-up things. Leave the finished sculptures in a cool, dry place for several days. Then have children observe how the clay changed.

Sand and Water Table

Sinking and Floating
Science

Materials: items that sink, such as stones, rubber balls, blocks; items that float, such as cork, sponges, toy boats

Demonstrate sinking by placing a "sinking" item in the water and having children observe what happens. Repeat this procedure for floating. Then have children look at the other items. Ask: **Which things will sink? Which things will float? Why do you think so?** Have children take turns placing the items in the water and observing what happens. Invite them to share observations.

Math Center

Measuring Juice   Math

Materials: apple juice, cranberry juice, grape juice, liquid measuring cup, large pitcher

Write the following recipe on the chalkboard. Read the juice labels for additives. You may wish to use picture icons for each type of fruit juice:

3 cups grape juice
3 cups apple juice
3 cups cranberry juice

Have children look at the juice and elicit from them that the juices are all liquids. Then display the measuring cup and have them predict what will happen to the juice when it is poured into the cup.

Measure one cup of juice for each child to pour into the pitcher. Once all the juice has been poured into the pitcher, stir and enjoy! **Caution: Check children's records for allergies.**

Technology Corner

The Red Balloon, Home Vision Cinema, 1956.

Sammy's Science House, Edmark.

School-Home Connection

Have children observe soda or other carbonated beverages with family members. Encourage them to use their senses of taste, touch, sound, and sight to find out about the gas bubbles in the liquid and how they behave.

Wrap Up and Assess

▶ Have children dictate to you all the solids, liquids, and gases they can find in the classroom, placing each in the correct category.

▶ Have each child make a collage showing solids or liquids by ripping or cutting out pictures of objects from old magazines. Encourage children to discuss their finished collages with classmates.

Portfolio   You may want to add **Activity Book** p. 28 to children's portfolios.

LESSON 15

Objectives

▶ **Investigate solids and liquids to find out how they can change.**

▶ **Predict what will happen to objects and substances as a result of change.**

Vocabulary

freeze	melt
cut	mix
fold	tear
change	

Process Skill

predict

Program Materials

Circle Time
Peanut Butter and Jelly
Big Book
Activity Time
Activity Book p. 29

Matter Changes

Circle Time

Invite children to tell about any experiences they have had cooking and to share some cooking words they know. Guide them to mention action words such as *cut, pour, mix,* and *bake.*

Display the **Big Book**. Then preview the pictures and ask children to **predict** what the book will be about.

Read through the book once, helping children track the print as you go. Reread the book, this time guiding children to do the hand motions as described on the last page. Then talk about the physical changes that were shown in the book. Ask: **What happened to the dough in the oven? What happened to the peanuts after they were cracked and mashed?**

Use Science Words

Vocabulary: freeze, melt, cut, mix, fold, tear, change

❶ Display a glass of water and tray of ice cubes. Have children share ideas about what *freezing* is. Ask: **What happens when water freezes? What makes water freeze?** Help them understand that frozen water is ice. The liquid water has *changed* to a solid. Then have them make a body motion to represent *freezing.* Ask: **Where can you find ice?**

❷ Have children share ideas about what *melting* is. Ask: **What makes snow or ice melt? What happens when it melts?** Help children understand that when snow or ice melts, it changes to liquid water. Have children make a body motion to represent *melting.*

❸ Talk about what happens to objects when they are cut. Then make up a hand motion to represent *cutting.* Repeat the procedure for *mixing.* You may also use this strategy to discuss other "change" words such as *folding* and *tearing.* Point out to children that freezing, melting, cutting, and mixing are all ways by which things are changed.

Activity Time

Have children recall what they learned about solids, liquids, and gases in the last lesson. Then hold up a sheet of paper and ask: **Is the paper a solid, a liquid, or a gas? How can you change the paper?** Invite them to suggest as many actions as possible, including cutting, tearing, folding, bending, and even wetting. List the words they suggest.

What makes an ice cube melt?

Materials: three ice cubes, two small plates, "warm" and "cool" labels, **Activity Book** p. 29

❶ Provide one of the ice cubes for children to examine. Ask: **How does the ice cube feel? What happens to it in your hand?** Place one ice cube on a plate labeled "warm" and another on a plate labeled "cool." Place the "warm" plate in a warm place and the "cool" plate in a cool place. Invite children to **predict** what will happen to each ice cube.

❷ Have children observe the ice cubes after 15 minutes. Ask: **What happened to the ice cubes?** Have them talk about their predictions and respond to the activity using **Activity Book** page 29.

Freezing

Materials: juice such as orange or apple, ice cube trays, craft sticks

Remind children that ice is frozen water. Then ask: **What other things can freeze? What makes them freeze?** Help children understand that cold can cause some liquids to freeze, or become solids.

To reinforce this concept, help children pour the juice into the ice cube trays. Then have them insert a craft stick into each cube of juice and **predict** what will happen if the juice gets very cold. Place the trays in a freezer overnight. The next day, have children observe the pops and discuss their predictions.

Science Background

The temperature at which a solid substance melts, or becomes a liquid, is called its *melting point*. Common cooking ingredients, such as butter or chocolate, melt at fairly low temperatures, while pure metals such as tungsten may be heated to temperatures of 3000° C (5432°F) before melting. The temperature at which different liquids freeze, or become solid, also varies. Fresh water typically freezes at 0° C (32°F), while alcohol, which was once used as antifreeze in cars, does not freeze until it reaches −130° C (−202°F).

Reaching All Learners

Extra Support Give children sheets of paper and encourage them to cut or tear the paper into as many different shapes as possible. Then have children compare their new shapes to an intact sheet of paper. Have children use concrete terms to talk about how the shape and size of the paper changed.

LESSON 15 Links

Reading Corner

▶ **Caring for Our Air** by Carol Greene, Enslow, 1991.

▶ **Everybody Cooks Rice** by Norah Dooley, Scott Foresman, 1992.

▶ **From Cow to Ice Cream** by Bertram T. Knight, Children's Press, 1997.

▶ **Joseph Had a Little Overcoat** by Simms Taback, Viking, 1999.

Language Arts Center

Make a Book
Language Arts

Materials: construction paper, drawing paper

Give each child one sheet of construction paper for a bookcover and two sheets of drawing paper for the pages of the book. Show them how to fold the pages in half. Talk about how you are changing the paper by folding it.

Suggest that children decorate the bookcover by changing the edges of the paper in some way, such as tearing them or cutting them. Let children tell how they changed their bookcovers. Then staple the pages together.

Social Studies Center

Popcorn
Social Studies

Materials: popcorn kernels, electric popcorn popper, bowl

Have children examine the unpopped corn kernels. Then ask: **How can we change this corn into popcorn?**

Heat the electric popper. Add the kernels and have children watch what happens. Explain that the heat cooked the kernels, causing them to pop. Children may want to act this out. **Caution: Before serving the popcorn, check children's records for allergy to corn.**

Art Center

Foil Art
Art

Materials: aluminum foil, paper plates, glue

Give each child a sheet of aluminum foil and ask: **How can you change the foil?** Demonstrate how the foil can be cut, rolled, twisted, and folded to create different effects.

Invite children to use foil to model objects such as animals, boats, cars, and people. Children may shape three-dimensional models from the foil or make flat pictures by gluing the foil onto the paper plates. Have children compare their work and talk about the strategies they used for changing the foil.

Sugar and Water

Science

Materials: clear cup of warm water, sugar, plastic spoon

Show children the sugar and point out that each granule is a solid. Ask: **What will happen to the sugar if I put it in the water?** Invite children to share their **predictions**. Then add one spoonful of sugar to the water, stir, and have children observe what happens.

Add one spoonful of sugar at a time, stirring well with each addition, until the sugar no longer dissolves in the water. Then give each child a plastic spoon with which to taste the sweet water. **Caution: Check for medical concerns.** Ask: **Where do you think the sugar went? Why do you think so?** You may want to extend this activity by trying the same thing with salt.

 Technology Corner

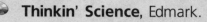 **Frosty the Snowman**, Sony.

Thinkin' Science, Edmark.

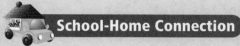 School-Home Connection

Invite family members to have children watch or help as they prepare meals at home. Encourage children to talk about the different ways foods are changed, for example, by heating and cooling, and to observe and discuss the effects of each change.

Wrap Up and Assess

▶ Stand in a circle and name a few "change" words for children such as *baking*, *tearing*, and *freezing*. Have each child suggest another change word.

▶ Have children make pictures from scrap craft materials they have torn, twisted, folded, glued, colored, wet, and changed in other ways.

Portfolio You may want to add **Activity Book** p. 29 to children's portfolios.

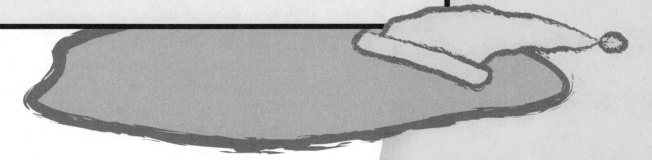

Objectives

▶ Understand that the way to change the position of an object is by pushing or pulling.

▶ Investigate various ways objects can move when pushed or pulled.

▶ Experiment with balancing objects.

Vocabulary

push   pull

Process Skill

investigate

Program Materials

Activity Time
    Kangaroo Surprise Little Book
    Activity Book p. 30

How Things Move

Circle Time

Can You?

Can you hop like a rabbit?   (Suit actions to words.)
Can you jump like a frog?
Can you walk like a duck?
Can you run like a dog?
Can you fly like a bird?
Can you swim like a fish?
Can you sit like a quiet child,
As still as this?

Have each child in the group name his or her favorite animal. Ask: **How does the animal get around?**

Read the rhyme "Can You?" with children, doing the actions that go with each line. Then reread the rhyme, having children do the actions along with you.

Extend the discussion to talk with children about the ways things move. Say: **You can jump up and down. You can walk back and forth. How else can you move?** Help children generate a list of ways things move, for example, "round and round," "in and out," and "zigzag."

Use Science Words

Vocabulary: push, pull

❶ Place a large object, such as a chair, in the circle. Ask: **How can we move the chair?** Elicit from children that one way to move the chair is to *push* it. Invite a volunteer to demonstrate. Then challenge children to name times when people push things, such as pushing a door to close it or pushing buttons on a phone or computer. List responses on the board under the word *Push*. Help children understand that *pushing* something often means moving it away from your body.

❷ Ask: **How else can we move the chair?** Then invite a volunteer to *pull* it. Talk with children about times when people pull things, such as pulling a door to open it or pulling a zipper to close a jacket. List responses on the board under the word *Pull*. Help children understand that *pulling* something often means moving it closer to your body.

Activity Time

Show the **Little Book** *Kangaroo Surprise* to children, read them the title, and have them predict what the book will be about. Read the book with small groups of children, tracking the print as you go. Have each group discuss the different types of movements shown.

How can we make objects move in different ways?

Materials: a variety of classroom objects such as square and cylindrical blocks, books, manipulatives, small cars; **Activity Book** p. 30

❶ Name a type of movement for children, such as back and forth, and have small groups **investigate** whether they can make the objects move back and forth by pushing or pulling.

❷ Repeat the procedure for other types of movement, such as straight, round and round, and zigzag. For each movement, have children tell whether a push or a pull worked for each object. Then ask them to complete **Activity Book** page 30.

Balancing

Materials: a ball; a balance; classroom manipulatives such as counters and small blocks

Explain to children that when an object falls, it is actually being pulled by Earth. Demonstrate this by holding a ball high up in the air and dropping it to the floor.

Then place a manipulative on one side of the balance. Have children observe that, the side with the object on it drops down. Then explain to children that they can keep the balance from tipping by placing another object that is about the same mass on the other side. This is called *balancing* the objects. Have children experiment with the manipulatives to find pairs of objects that balance.

Anything that makes an object move is a *force*. *Gravity* is an important force in the universe. Gravitational pull is what causes Earth's circular path around the sun and the moon's circular path around Earth. Gravity also pulls on objects and living things on Earth. Gravity is what causes objects to fall to the ground when dropped.

Reaching All Learners

Challenge Have children use crayons and paper to make lines that show ways of moving, such as "round and round," "zigzag," and "straight."

LESSON 16 Links

Reading Corner

- ▶ **The Great Big Enormous Turnip** by Alexei Tolstoi, Franklin Watts, 1968.
- ▶ **Farmer Brown Goes Round and Round** by Teri Sloat, DK Pub Merchandise, 2001.
- ▶ **Silly Sally** by Audrey Wood, Harcourt, 1992.
- ▶ **Wheel Away!** by Dayle Ann Dodds, HarperCollins, 1989.

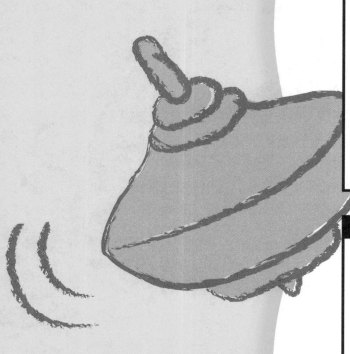

Block Center

Block Ramps   Science

Materials: blocks from the Block Center or cardboard boxes, toy cars

Point out to children that objects can move fast or slowly when pushed or pulled. Ask: **How can you make something move faster or more slowly?** Help children understand that often a harder push or pull will make an object move faster.

Then have children build long ramps, short ramps, steep ramps, and low ramps with the blocks. Ask: **Will the ramp make the cars move faster or more slowly?** Invite children to investigate which ramps help the cars move the fastest.

Then ask: **What will happen if you put one car at the bottom of a ramp and roll another car down the ramp?** Have children investigate to find out what happens and then tell whether the resulting movement was a push or a pull.

Movement Center

Simon Says   Movement

Play a game of "Simon Says" with children, instructing them to move in different ways. For example, you might ask them to:

- • **Turn round and round.**
- • **Jump up and down.**
- • **March in a straight line.**
- • **Move your arms round and round.**

Dramatic Play Center

Explore Tools   Science

Materials: play tools such as hammers, saws, screwdrivers

Talk with children about how people use pushing and pulling to build things. Then explain that tools can make this work easier. Invite children to extend their understanding of pushing and pulling by exploring the tools in the Dramatic Play Center.

Music Center

Sing a Movement Song

Music

Sing the first verse of "The Wheels on the Bus" with children:

The wheels on the bus go round and round,
Round and round, round and round
The wheels on the bus go round and round,
All through the town.

Then sing additional verses, replacing "The wheels on the bus" and "round and round" with descriptions of how other parts of the bus move. Possibilities include:

The wipers on the bus go back and forth…
The door on the bus goes open and shut…
The children on the bus bounce up and down.

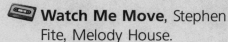

Watch Me Move, Stephen Fite, Melody House.

Stickybear's Early Learning Activities, Sunburst.

School-Home Connection

Have children talk with family members about toys they play with at home. Encourage them to discuss how each toy moves and whether a push or pull is required to play with it. Suggest that they also discuss pushes and pulls as used in sports.

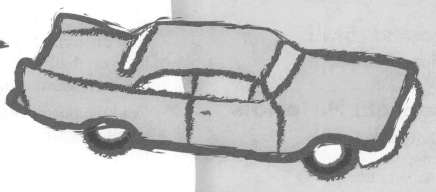

Wrap Up and Assess

▶ Have children take turns finding something in the classroom they can push or pull. They can demonstrate the movement for others.

▶ Have each child practice pushing and pulling using clay. If possible, provide rollers for children to use as they work with the clay.

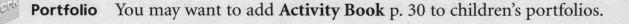

Portfolio You may want to add **Activity Book** p. 30 to children's portfolios.

Objectives

▶ Observe through simple explorations how magnets work.

▶ Experiment with magnets to find out what objects they attract.

Vocabulary

attract   magnet

Process Skill

compare

Program Materials

Activity Time
    magnet
    Activity Book p. 31
Links
    magnet

Magnets

Circle Time

A Tour

On our refrigerator door
Is where my best things go.
I put up on it anything
I really want to show.
A worksheet from my class at school,
A photograph of me,
A ribbon from a race I ran,
A painting of a tree.
Here's a picture of my dog,
And here's my best friend, Sue.
I use these letters to make my name.
Can you make your name, too?

Introduce children to magnets by having them tell about things they hang on their refrigerators at home. Ask: **What things do you put on your refrigerator door? How do you get them to stay on it?**

Read the poem with children and then extend the discussion to talk about magnets. Ask: **What is a magnet? What do magnets do?** If there are any magnets being used in your classroom, such as magnets on cabinet doors, point them out.

Use Science Words

Vocabulary: attract, magnet

❶ Provide children with a variety of magnets to explore. Then say: **These are all magnets. What is the same about them all?** Have children discuss their observations.

❷ Demonstrate attaching a metal object, such as a paper clip, to one of the magnets. Explain that magnets can attract some things. Then ask: **What do you think *attract* means?** If necessary, demonstrate the paper clip being attracted to the magnet again. Have children formulate a definition for *attract*.

Activity Time

Invite children to examine your collection of magnets more closely. Lead them in a discussion of how the magnets are alike and different, **comparing** the sizes, shapes, and thicknesses of the magnets.

 **Investigate**

What can a magnet attract?

Materials: magnet; small metal and non-metal objects such as paper clips, rubber balls, screws, toy cars; **Activity Book** p. 31

❶ Place the **magnet** and small objects together on a table. Have children locate the magnet and tell how they identified it.

❷ Have children experiment to find out which objects the magnet will attract and which it will not. Invite them to sort the objects into two groups: things the magnet will attract and things the magnet will not attract. Have them record their findings on **Activity Book** page 31.

❸ Lead children in a discussion **comparing** the two groups of objects. Help them notice that the items attracted by the magnet are all made of a metal called iron.

 **Learn About**

A Magnet's Poles

Materials: large bar magnet, small paper clips

Explain to children that a magnet's pull is stronger in some places than others. Have them share ideas, based on prior observations, about where a magnet's pull might be strongest.

Have children wave the bar magnet over and close to the pile of paper clips several times and observe what happens. Elicit from them that the magnet's pull is strongest at its two ends. Explain that the parts of a magnet where its pull is strongest are called its *poles*.

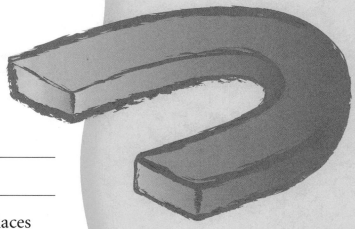

LESSON 17 Links

Reading Corner

▶ **Magnetism** by John Woodruff, Steck-Vaughn, 1998.

▶ **Magnets and Sparks** by Wendy Madgwick, Steck-Vaughn, 1999.

▶ **Mr. Fixit's Magnet Machine** by Richard Scarry, Simon Spotlight, 1998.

▶ **What Magnets Can Do** by Allan Fowler, Children's Press, 1995.

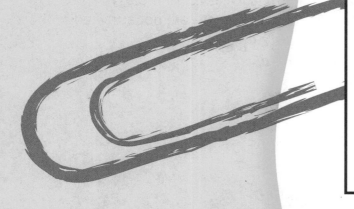

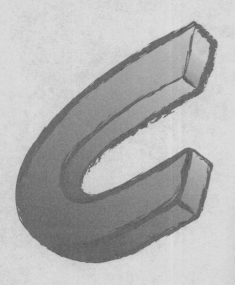

Magnetic Words

Language Arts

Materials: cookie sheets, magnetic letters, index cards

Write each child's name on an index card and place the cards in the Language Arts Center. Help each child locate his or her name among the cards. Then have children use the cards as models for forming their own names on the cookie sheets with magnetic letters. You may wish to have more advanced learners practice forming other words as well. They may want to start with family names.

Make a Magnet Toy

Science

Materials: shoe-box lids, crayons, metal toy car, **magnet**

Have children use crayons to draw a road or race course on the shoe-box lid; make sure the rim of the lid is facing up. (You may want to make a template of the course for children to use.) Encourage them to include scenery such as trees, buildings, or even people. Then show them how they can run the **magnet** underneath the lid to pull the car around inside the scene.

Compare Magnet Pulls

Math

Materials: interlocking cubes, a variety of magnets, paper clip, chart paper

Make a tall bar of interlocking cubes and stand it up straight. Place the paper clip next to the bottom of the stack. Have children experiment to find out how many cubes high one of the magnets can be lifted before it stops pulling the clip. Repeat this procedure for other magnets.

What Can a Magnet Pull Through?

Science

Materials: magnet; paper clip; scraps of various art materials such as cardboard, construction paper, fabric, or acetate

Explain to children that some magnets are strong enough to pull through other things. Demonstrate by pulling the paper clip on top of a sheet of paper by moving a **magnet** underneath.

Have children try pulling the paper clip with the magnet through other materials. For materials that the magnet can pull through easily, you may then want to have children try pulling through few or many layers. Talk about which materials the magnet could pull through and which it could not.

Technology Corner

 Sammy's Science House, Edmark.

 Stickybear's Early Learning Activities, Sunburst.

School-Home Connection

Encourage families to set up spaces on their refrigerators where children can work with magnets. You may suggest that children can also use these spaces to hang drawings and other schoolwork they wish to share with family members.

Wrap Up and Assess

▶ Share with children some of the practical uses for magnets, such as in toys, hanging papers, keeping things closed, and even sorting trash. Have children brainstorm other uses for magnets based on what they have learned.

▶ Have each child draw a magnet attracting something. Show a sample drawing. Encourage children to show the magnets attracting things that they actually do attract. Label the drawings.

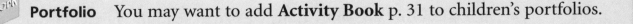

My Work

Portfolio   You may want to add **Activity Book** p. 31 to children's portfolios.

Objectives

▶ **Experiment with simple machines to find out how they make jobs easier.**

▶ **Construct simple machines that push or pull other objects.**

▶ **Understand that electricity is energy that helps some machines do work.**

Vocabulary

machine   tool

Process Skill

investigate

Program Materials

Activity Time
    Activity Book p. 32
Links
    hand lens

Simple Machines

Circle Time

One wheel, two wheels, on the ground   (Revolve hands in circle to illustrate wheels.)

My feet make the pedals go round and round.   (Move feet in pedaling motion.)

Handle bars help me steer so straight,   (Pretend to steer bicycle.)

Down the sidewalk, through the gate.

Lead children in a conversation about wheels. Ask: **What do wheels look like? What shape are they? Where can you find wheels?** Have children discuss cars, bicycles, trains, wagons, wheelchairs, and other wheeled vehicles, helping them notice that wheels are often found on things that help people go places.

Read the motion rhyme to children, acting out the motions that go with each line. Then read it again, having children complete the motions with you. Invite them to talk about bicycles they have ridden or seen.

Then ask: **What would happen if you took the wheels off a bicycle?** Elicit from children that without its wheels, a bicycle would not move.

Use Science Words

Vocabulary: machine, tool

❶ Talk with children about machines and tools in their everyday world. Explain: *Machines* **and** *tools* **are things that help us do work. They make work easier. What machines and tools do you know that make work easier?** Help children identify computers, building and carpentry equipment, cooking utensils, and so on.

❷ Then ask: **What are some tools we use in school?** Have children scan the classroom for tools such as scissors, forks and spoons, rulers, and science equipment such as hand lenses or scales. List the words on the board. Then label the tools in the classroom with words from the list.

Activity Time

Display a variety of classroom tools and simple machines for children to examine. Hold up each one, identify it, and ask: **What do we use this for?** Then ask: **What would happen if we didn't use [name of object] to [description of task]?** Help children understand that each machine or tool makes a task easier.

What can we use to move an object?

Materials: large book; construction items such as yarn, rubber bands, blocks, cardboard; scissors; **Activity Book** p. 32

1 Mark two spots in the room as "Start" and "Finish," making sure there is a straight path between them. Tell children that they are to move the book from Start to Finish without touching it with their bodies. Model one way to move the book.

2 Have children **investigate** how to move the book using the construction materials provided. Be sure that they do not use their bodies to transport the book directly. Invite each group to demonstrate its solution. Then have children complete **Activity Book** page 32.

Electricity

Materials: index cards, tape, markers

Point out to children any lamps, computers, or other classroom machines that plug into the wall. Tell them that these machines need a form of energy, called *electricity*, to work. People plug these machines into electrical outlets in the wall to give them electricity.

Talk with children about electricity and safety. Make a special icon, such as a hand with an "X" through it, and explain that this is the "Don't Touch!" sign. Draw the icon on index cards and tape them next to electrical sockets and electrical machines around the room.

People use many simple machines to do work. Some of the most common simple machines are *levers*, used to lift and open things; *pulleys*, often used to lift things; *ramps*, which help objects move more easily; *wedges*, which help push or split things apart; *wheels* and *axles*, which help tighten or turn; and *screws*, which can sometimes be used to lift objects up or pry them apart.

Reaching All Learners

ESL Have children make collages by cutting out pictures of carpentry tools and machines from old magazines. Once the collages are complete, tell children the names of the different items pictured and have them practice saying the names aloud.

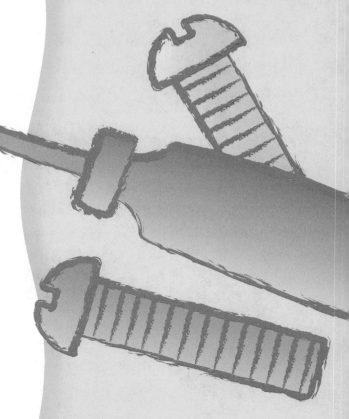

LESSON 18 Links

Reading Corner

▶ **Construction Zone** by Tana Hoban, Greenwillow, 1999.

▶ **I Spy Little Wheels** by Jean Marzollo, Scholastic, 1998.

▶ **Machines at Work** by Byron Barton, HarperCollins, 1997.

▶ **Tool Book** by Gail Gibbons, Holiday House, 1988.

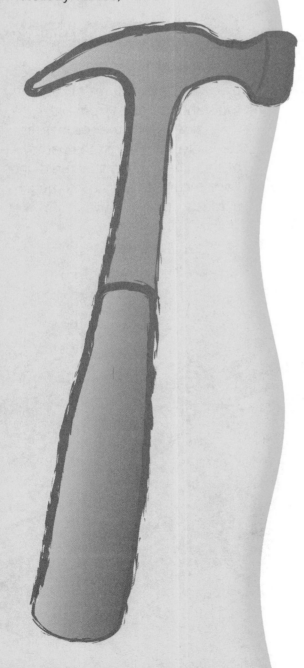

Table Top Center

A Closer Look at Moving Parts

Science

Materials: hand lens; screwdriver; pliers; discarded non-working household machines such as telephones, cameras, typewriters, wind-up alarm clocks

Use the screwdriver and pliers to take the bottoms or backs off the machines. Supervise children closely as they examine the inner workings of each machine, using a **hand lens** when necessary. Have them talk about the different parts they observe and tinker with the machines carefully to find out how some of their parts move. **Caution: Tell children not to put any part of the machines near their faces.**

House Center

Explore Kitchen Tools

Science

Materials: kitchen tools for use in the House Center

Bring in a variety of child-safe kitchen tools and simple machines such as a handheld can opener, wire whisk, wooden spoons, and measuring cups. Lead children in a discussion about what each one is used for and how it works. Then place the objects in the House Center for children to explore.

Outdoors Center

Take a Wheel Walk

Science

Take children on a walk around the school and school grounds in search of objects with wheels. Talk about how the wheels help the different objects move. Also invite children to observe which vehicles move fast, which move slowly, which ones people push or pull, and which ones people drive.

Social Studies Center

Cleaning Up, Long Ago and Today
Social Studies

Materials: cut-out pictures of household cleaning machines such as washing machines and vacuum cleaners; crayons; drawing paper

Display the pictures for children and talk about the machines shown. Invite volunteers to name the different machines, tell what they do and how people operate them, and discuss the sounds they make.

Then explain to children that long ago, people did not have these machines. Ask: **How do you think people got dirt off the floor without a vacuum? How did they wash clothes without a washing machine?** Talk about people cleaning without the help of modern-day machines. (The Internet may provide ideas and pictures for this.) Then discuss whether they think life was easier long ago or whether it is easier today.

Technology Corner

 Bob the Builder— Can We Fix It?, Lyrick Studios, 2001.

 I Love Big Machines, Consumervision, 1994.

School-Home Connection

Have children and family members look around their homes together for tools and machines. Encourage them to talk about what each object does, how it is used, and what job it makes easier.

Wrap Up and Assess

► Have each child in the group dramatize using a tool or machine to do work. Have other children guess what object is being shown and discuss the task it helps a person do.

► Provide children with crayons and drawing paper and invite them to draw tools or machines they use often. Label the pictures. Hang all pictures on the wall as a "Tools We Use" display.

Portfolio You may want to add **Activity Book** p. 32 to children's portfolios.

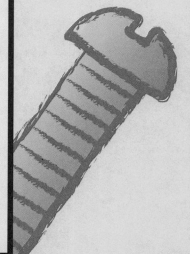